THE PLAYLIST
CHORD SONG

This publication is not authorised for sale in the United States of America and / or Canada

WISE PUBLICATIONS
part of The Music Sales Group
London / New York / Paris / Sydney / Copenhagen / Berlin / Madrid / Tokyo

Published by
Wise Publications
14-15 Berners Street, London, W1T 3LJ, UK.

Exclusive distributors:
Music Sales Limited, Distribution Centre, Newmarket Road,
Bury St Edmunds, Suffolk, IP33 3YR, UK.
Music Sales Pty Limited
20 Resolution Drive, Caringbah, NSW 2229, Australia.

Order No. AM994235
ISBN 978-1-84772-609-4
This book © Copyright 2008 Wise Publications,
a division of Music Sales Limited.

Unauthorised reproduction of any part of this publication by
any means including photocopying is an infringement of copyright.

Music arranged by Martin Shellard.
Compiled by Nick Crispin.
Edited by Sam Harrop.

Printed in the EU.

www.musicsales.com

Your Guarantee of Quality:
As publishers, we strive to produce every book
to the highest commercial standards.

The music has been freshly engraved and the book has been
carefully designed to minimise awkward page turns and to make
playing from it a real pleasure. Particular care has been given
to specifying acid-free, neutral-sized paper made from pulps
which have not been elemental chlorine bleached.

This pulp is from farmed sustainable forests and
was produced with special regard for the environment.

Throughout, the printing and binding have been planned
to ensure a sturdy, attractive publication which should give
years of enjoyment.

If your copy fails to meet our high standards, please inform us
and we will gladly replace it.

AFTER HOURS WE ARE SCIENTISTS 4
ALWAYS WHERE I NEED TO BE THE KOOKS 7
A-PUNK VAMPIRE WEEKEND 10
BLEED IT OUT LINKIN PARK 12
CAN'T GET ALONG (WITHOUT YOU) HARD-FI 16
CHARMER KINGS OF LEON 22
CHASING PAVEMENTS ADELE 19
DIG, LAZARUS, DIG!!! NICK CAVE & THE BAD SEEDS 24
DOG HOUSE BOOGIE SEASICK STEVE 30
FLOODS FIGHTSTAR 28
FOLDING STARS BIFFY CLYRO 33
GILT COMPLEX SONS & DAUGHTERS 36
GREAT DJ THE TING TINGS 39
I'M A REALIST THE CRIBS 42
I'M LIKE A LAWYER WITH THE WAY I'M ALWAYS TRYING TO GET YOU OFF (ME & YOU) FALL OUT BOY 45
INDIAN SUMMER MANIC STREET PREACHERS 48
IT MEANS NOTHING STEREOPHONICS 51
JUST FOR TONIGHT ONE NIGHT ONLY 54
THE KILL THIRTY SECONDS TO MARS 57
LONG ROAD TO RUIN FOO FIGHTERS 63
LORD DON'T SLOW ME DOWN OASIS 60
LOVE'S NOT A COMPETITION (BUT I'M WINNING) KAISER CHIEFS 66
MAKE IT WIT CHU QUEENS OF THE STONE AGE 68
MERCY DUFFY 70
MOUTHWASH KATE NASH 73
MOVING TO NEW YORK THE WOMBATS 76
PAPER PLANES M.I.A. 78
PUSH YOUR HEAD TOWARDS THE AIR EDITORS 80
ROMANTIC TYPE THE PIGEON DETECTIVES 82
RUN GNARLS BARKLEY 84
THE STEP AND THE WALK THE DUKE SPIRIT 87
STRANGE TIMES THE BLACK KEYS 90
TEARDROP NEWTON FAULKNER 92
TELL ME WHAT IT'S WORTH LIGHTSPEED CHAMPION 94
THAT'S HOW PEOPLE GROW UP MORRISSEY 96
TIME TO PRETEND MGMT 98
TRANQUILIZE THE KILLERS FEAT. LOU REED 101
VALENTINE RICHARD HAWLEY 104
WHAT WILL YOU DO (WHEN THE MONEY GOES)? MILBURN 106
WORRIED ABOUT RAY THE HOOSIERS 110

After Hours

Words & Music by
Keith Murray & Christopher Cain

| E | Asus2 | C#m7 | Badd11 | A | F# | F#m7 |

Intro ‖: E | E :‖ *play 4 times*

Verse 1
   E
 This door is always open,

This door is always open,
Asus2   E
No-one has the guts to shut us out.

But if we have to go now,

I guess there's always hope that,
Asus2   E
Some place will be serving after hours.

Chorus 1
 C#m7   **Badd11**
  This night is winding down,
 E
But time means nothing.
 C#m7   **Badd11**
  As always at this hour,
 E
Time means nothing.
 C#m7   **Badd11**
  One final, final round,
    E   **Asus2**
'Cause time means nothing,
     E **Asus2**   E
Say that you'll stay, say that you'll stay.

© Copyright 2008 Sony/ATV Music Publishing (UK) Limited.
All Rights Reserved. International Copyright Secured.

Interlude 1   ‖: E | E   :‖

　　　　　　| Asus² | Asus² |

　　　　　　| E | E |

Verse 2
　　　　　　E
　　　　　　　We're finally drunk enough that,

　　　　We're finally soaking up,
　　　　　　Asus²   E
　　　　The hours that everyone else throws a - way.

　　　　And if we have to go now,

　　　　I guess there's always hope,
　　　　　　Asus²   E
　　　　To - morrow night will be more of the same.

Chorus 2
　　　　C♯m⁷   Badd¹¹
　　　　　　This night is winding down,
　　　　　　E
　　　　But time means nothing.
　　　　C♯m⁷   Badd¹¹
　　　　　　As always at this hour,
　　　　E
　　　　Time means nothing.
　　　　C♯m⁷   Badd¹¹
　　　　　　One final, final round,
　　　　　　E   Asus²
　　　　'Cause time means nothing.
　　　　　　　　E   Asus²
　　　　Say that you'll stay,
　　　　　　　　E   Asus²
　　　　Say that you'll stay,
　　　　　　　　E
　　　　Say that you'll stay.

Interlude 2 ‖: E | E :‖ *play 4 times*

Bridge
        A
We're alright where we're supposed to be.
       F♯
We're alright where we're supposed to be.
       A   **F♯m7**
We're alright where we're sup - posed to be.
       A   **F♯m7**
We're alright where we're sup - posed to be

Link ‖: E | E :‖

Verse 3
E
This door is always open,

This door is always open,
Asus2   **E**   **Asus2**
No-one has the guts to shut us out.
                         E
No-one has the guts to shut us out.

Chorus 3
E/C♯ **E/B** **E**
       Time means nothing,
E/C♯ **E/B** **E**
       Time means nothing.
E/C♯   **E/B**
   One final, final round,
     E   **Asus2**
'Cause time means nothing.
           E **Asus2**
Say that you'll stay,
           E **Asus2**
Say that you'll stay,
        E
Say that you'll stay.

Outro ‖: E | E :‖ *play 4 times*

Always Where I Need To Be

Words & Music by
Luke Pritchard

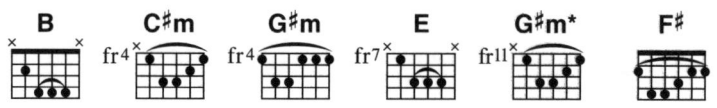

Intro ‖: B | B   C♯m |
         | G♯m | G♯m   E   :‖ play 3 times

Verse 1
```
         B                C♯m  G♯m
         She don't know who she   is,
                           E     B
         Oh, I can take her any - where.
                  C♯m    G♯m
         Do whatever comes naturally to you.
                                E
         You know she just don't  care,
                           B
         You know she just don't  care.
```

Chorus 1
```
                       E           G♯m*
         'Cause I am always where I need to be,
                 E
         And I always thought,
                 G♯m*              B
         I would end up with you eventual - ly.
                           C♯m
         Doo, do-do, doo, do-do,
         G♯m                 E
         Doo, doo, do-do, doo, do-do,
         B                    C♯m
         Doo, doo, do-do, doo, do-do,
         G♯m
         Doo.
```

© 2007 Famous Music LLC.
Famous Music Publishing Limited.
All Rights Reserved. International Copyright Secured.

Verse 2

	B	C♯m G♯m

Now I see her a - gain,

                      E   B
I asked to be a hum - ming - bird.

                    C♯m G♯m
Whisper words in her   ear,

                              E
Oh, now you know I just don't   care,

                     B
You know she just don't   care.

Chorus 2

           E   G♯m*
'Cause I am always where I need to be,

    E
And I always thought,

          G♯m*   B
I would end up with you eventual - ly.

                  C♯m
Doo, do-do, doo, do-do,

G♯m   E
Doo, doo, do-do, doo, do-do,

B   C♯m
Doo, doo, do-do, doo, do-do,

G♯m
    Say!

Guitar solo

‖: B | B   C♯m |

| G♯m | G♯m   E :‖

8

Bridge   **E**
        Oh Lord, I'm a man on,
      G♯m*
          Oh, I'm a man on the scene,
     E   **G♯m***
       I'm a man and I can   be so obscene.

Chorus 3
           E   **G♯m***
Because I   always think that I know   how to be,
     E
But I always thought,
         G♯m*   **F♯**   **B**
I would end up with you   eventual - ly.
           C♯m
Doo, do-do, doo, do-do,
G♯m   **E**
Doo, doo, do-do, doo, do-do,
B   **C♯m**
Doo, doo, do-do, doo, do-do,
G♯m
    Say!

Outro   **E**
        Oh Lord, I'm a man on,
     G♯m*
          Oh, I'm a man on the scene,
     E
      I'm a man, I'm a man,
G♯m*   **B**
    I can be so ob - scene.

A-Punk

Words & Music by
Christopher Baio, Rostam Batmanglij, Ezra Koenig & Christopher Tomson

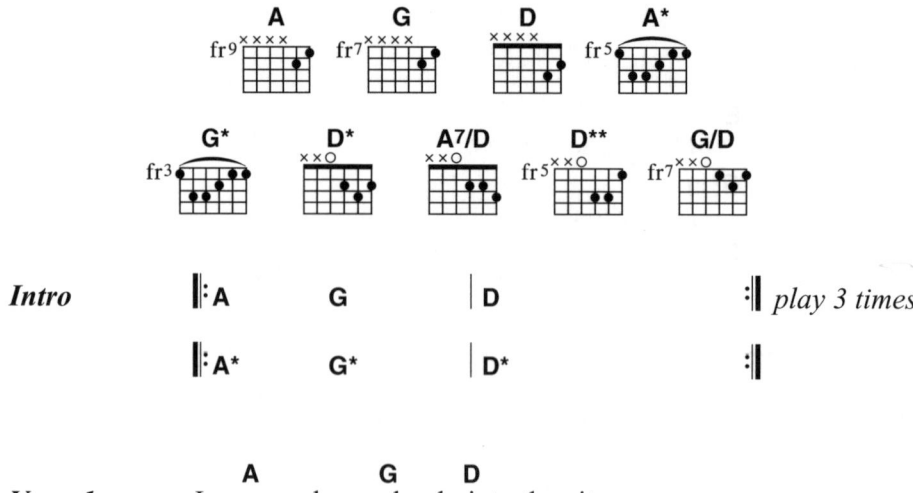

Intro

‖: A   G | D   :‖ *play 3 times*

‖: A*   G* | D*   :‖

Verse 1

        A   G   D
Jo - anna drove slowly into the city,
       A   G   D
The Hudson River all filled with snow,
       A   G   D
She spied the ring on his honour finger,
A*   G*   D*   A*   G*   D*
Oh, oh, oh.
       A   G   D
A thousand years in one piece of silver,
     A   G   D
She took it from his lily-white hand,
   A   G   D
Showed no fear she'd seen the thing,
       A*   G*   D*   A*   G*   D*
In the young men's wing at Sloan-Kettering.

Link 1

| D   A7/D   D**   D | G/D   D**   D |

| D   A7/D   D**   D | G/D   D** |

Chorus 1

D   A7/D   D**   D   G/D
Look out - side at the raincoats coming, say oh!

© Copyright 2007 Zomba Music Publishers Limited.
All Rights Reserved. International Copyright Secured.

Link 2

    A G D
         Hey! Hey! Hey! Hey!
    A G D
         Hey! Hey! Hey!

Verse 2

      A   G   D
His honor drove southward seeking exotica,
  A   G   D
Down to the Pueblo huts of New Mexico,
  A   G   D
Cut his teeth on turquoise harmonicas,
  A* G* D* A* G* D*
Oh, oh, oh.
  A   G   D
I saw Jo - anna down in the subway,
     A   G   D
She took an a - partment in Washington Heights,
  A   G   D
Half of the ring lies here with me,
     A*   G*   D*   A* G* D*
But the other half's at the bottom of the sea.

Link 3

| D A7/D D** D | G/D   D** D |

| D A7/D D** D | G/D   D** |

Chorus 2

D   A7/D   D**   D   G/D D** D
Look outside at the raincoats coming, say oh!
D   A7/D   D**   D   G/D D**
Look outside at the raincoats coming, say oh!
D   A7/D   D**   D   G/D D** D
Look outside at the raincoats coming, say oh!
D   A7/D   D**   D   G/D
Look outside at the raincoats coming, say oh!

Outro

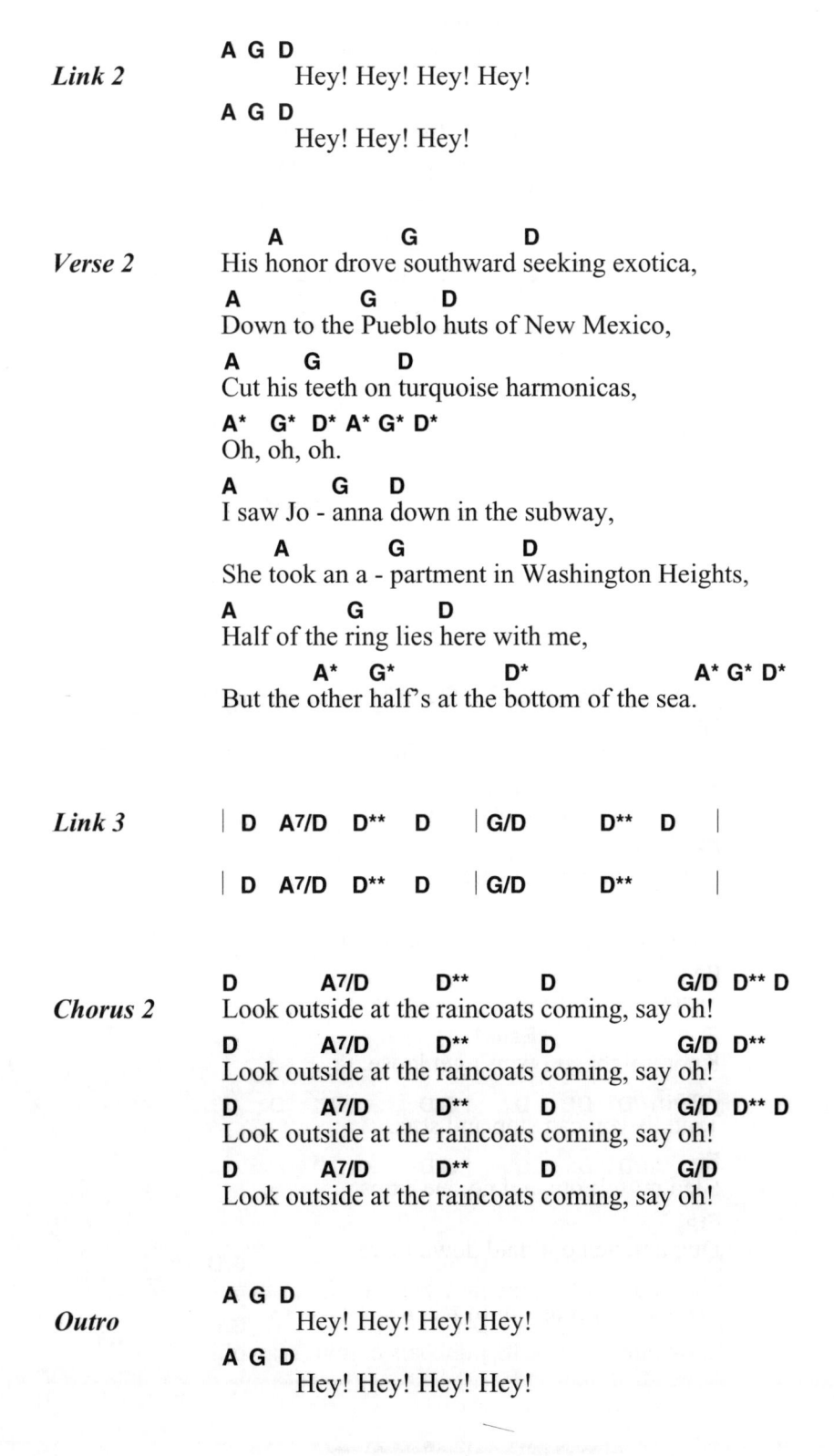

    A G D
         Hey! Hey! Hey! Hey!
    A G D
         Hey! Hey! Hey! Hey!

Bleed It Out

Words & Music by
Chester Bennington, Mike Shinoda, Rob Bourdon,
Brad Delson, Dave Farrell & Joe Hahn

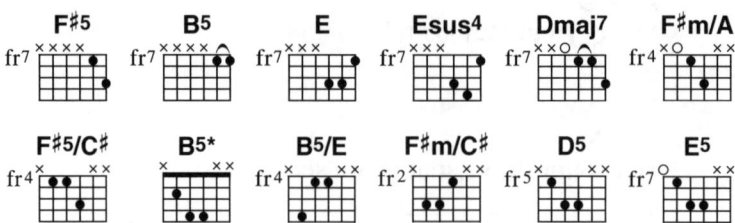

Intro | F#5 | F#5 |
            | B5 | E   Esus4 |

Verse 1
F#5
Here we go for the hundredth time,

Hand grenade pins in every line,
B5
Throw 'em up and let somethin' shine,
E   Esus4
Going out of my fuckin' mind.
F#5
Filthy mouth, no excuse,

Find a new place to hang this noose,
B5
String me up from atop these roofs,
E   Esus4
Knot it tight so I won't get loose.
Dmaj7
Truth is you can stop and stare,
E
Bled myself out and no one cares,
F#5
Dug a trench out, laid down there,

With a shovel up out of reach somewhere.

© Copyright 2007 Zomba Music Publishers Limited.
All Rights Reserved. International Copyright Secured.

cont.

Dmaj7
Yeah someone pour it in,
E
Make it a dirt dance floor again,
B5
Say your prayers and stomp it out,
      E   **Esus4**
When they bring that chorus in.

Chorus 1

  F♯5*
I bleed it out,
        F♯m/A **F♯5/C♯**
Digging deeper just to throw it a - way.
B5*
I bleed it out,
       B5/E   **F♯m/C♯**
Digging deeper just to throw it a - way.
  F♯5*
I bleed it out,
        F♯m/A **F♯5/C♯**
Digging deeper just to throw it a - way,
  B5*   **B5/E**   **F♯m/C♯**
Just to throw it away, just to throw it a - way.
  F♯5
I bleed it out,

Verse 2

F♯5
Go, stop the show,

Choppy words and a sloppy flow.
B5
Shotgun opera, lock and load,
E   **Esus4**
Cock it back and then watch it go.
F♯5
Mama help me, I've been cursed,

Death is rolling in every verse,
B5
Candy paint on his brand new hearse,
E   **Esus4**
Can't contain him, he knows he works.

13

cont.

    Dmaj⁷
Fuck this hurts, I won't lie,
E
Doesn't matter how hard I try,
F♯5
Half the words don't mean a thing,

And I know that I won't be satisfied.
    Dmaj⁷
So why   try ignoring him,
E
Make it a dirt dance floor again,
B5
Say your prayers and stomp it out,
      E   **Esus⁴**
When they bring that chorus in.

Chorus 2   As Chorus 1

Bridge

D5   **E5**
I've opened up these scars,
           D5
I'll make you face this.
       E5
I pulled myself so far,
      D5 **E5** (**F♯5**)
I'll make you face this now.

Interlude | F♯5 | F♯5 |
               (now.)
               | B5 | E   Esus4 |

Chorus 3
                   F♯5
             I bleed it out,

             Digging deeper just to throw it away.
                B5
             I bleed it out,
                                     E   Esus4
             Digging deeper just to throw it a - way.
                 F♯5
             I bleed it out,

             Digging deeper just to throw it away,
                B5   E   Esus4
             Just to throw it away, just to throw it a - way.

Chorus 4   As Chorus 1

Outro
                   F♯5* F♯m/A F♯5/C♯
             I bleed it out,
             B5* B5/E F♯m/C♯   F♯5* F♯m/A F♯5/C♯
                        I bleed it out,
             B5* B5/E F♯m/C♯   F♯5*
                        I bleed it out.

Can't Get Along (Without You)

Words & Music by
Richard Archer

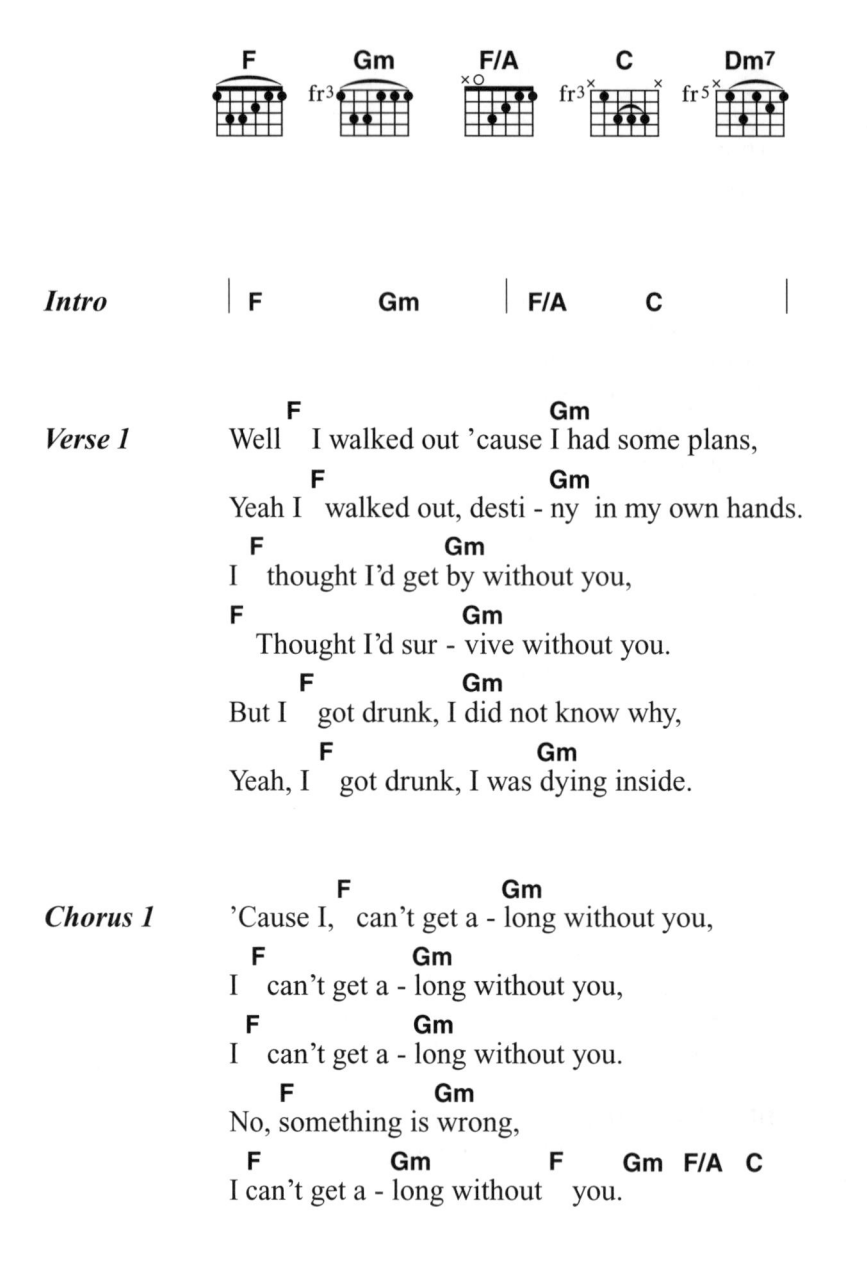

F   Gm   F/A   C   Dm7

Intro | F   Gm | F/A   C |

Verse 1
         F   Gm
Well   I walked out 'cause I had some plans,
       F   Gm
Yeah I   walked out, desti - ny in my own hands.
    F   Gm
I   thought I'd get by without you,
F   Gm
Thought I'd sur - vive without you.
      F   Gm
But I   got drunk, I did not know why,
        F   Gm
Yeah, I   got drunk, I was dying inside.

Chorus 1
        F   Gm
'Cause I,   can't get a - long without you,
  F   Gm
I   can't get a - long without you,
  F   Gm
I   can't get a - long without you.
    F   Gm
No, something is wrong,
  F   Gm   F   Gm F/A C
I   can't get a - long without   you.

© Copyright 2002 Universal Music Publishing MGB.
All Rights in Germany Administered by Musik Edition Discoton GmbH
(A Division of Universal Music Publishing Group).
All Rights Reserved. International Copyright Secured.

Verse 2

        F   Gm
So, I   picked fights, with men twice my size,
         F   Gm
Yeah, I   picked fights, they punched out my lights.
         F   Gm
And I,   I took smack so I   could get high,
F   Gm
  I got hooked and I nearly died.
        F   Gm
And I,   I slept rough, I lived on the streets,
        F   Gm
Yeah I,   I slept rough, news - paper for sheets.

Chorus 2

          F   Gm
'Cause I, I can't get a - long without you,
    F   Gm
I   can't get a - long without you,
    F   Gm
I   can't get a - long without you.
     F   Gm
No, something is wrong,
    F   Gm   F   Gm F/A C
I can't get a - long without   you.

Interlude

  Dm7
‖:   Ooh, ooh, ooh-hoo,

Ooh, ooh, ooh-hoo, ooh. :‖

Verse 3

      F   **Gm**
So, I got a train and I headed home,
       F   **Gm**
Yeah, I, I got a train to the town I was born.
       F   **Gm**
And I went back to the place where we'd meet,
F   **N.C.**
I broke down and cried in the street.
        F   **Gm**
'Cause I realised what I'd done wrong,
     F   **N.C.**
Yeah I, I fucked up, I loved you all along.

Chorus 3

  F   **Gm**
Can't get a - long without you,
   F   **Gm**
I can't get a - long without you,
  F   **Gm**   **F** **Gm F/A**
I can't get a - long without you, girl.
    C   **F**   **Gm**
Believe me baby, can't get a - long without you,
  F   **Gm**
I can't get a - long without you,
  F   **Gm**
I can't get a - long without you.
   F   **Gm**
No, something is wrong,
  F   **Gm**   **F** **Gm**
I can't get a - long without you.
F/A   **C**
I really need you, baby.

18

Chasing Pavements

Words & Music by
Francis White & Adele Adkins

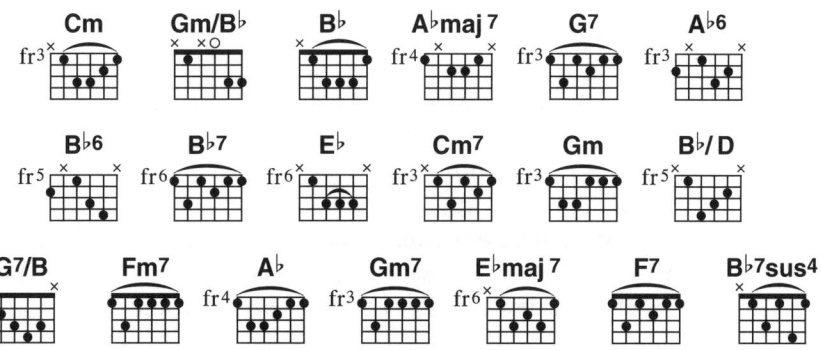

Intro | Cm | Gm/B♭   B♭ |

Verse 1
    Cm
I've made up my mind,
    Gm/B♭   **B♭**
Don't need to think it over,
    A♭maj7
If I'm wrong, I am right,
    G7
Don't need to look no further,
    A♭6 **B♭6** **B♭7** **E♭** **Cm7**
This ain't lust, I know this is love.

Verse 2
    Gm **E♭**
But if I tell the world,
    B♭/D
I'll never say enough,
    Cm
'Cause it was not said to you,
    G7/B **G7**
And that's ex - actly what I need to do,
    A♭6 **B♭6** **B♭7**
If I end up   with you.

© Copyright 2007 Universal Music Publishing Limited.
All rights in Germany administered by Universal Music Publ. GmbH.
All Rights Reserved. International Copyright Secured.

Chorus 1

A♭maj7
Should I give up,
Gm Cm   Fm7   A♭
  Or should I just keep chasing pavements?
A♭6   Gm7   G7
Even if it leads no - where?
    A♭maj7   Gm
Or would it be a waste,
Cm Fm7   A♭   A♭6   G7
Even if I knew my place, should I leave it there?
A♭maj7
Should I give up,
Gm Cm   Fm7   A♭
  Or should I just keep chasing pavements?
A♭6   Gm7   E♭maj7
Even if it leads nowhere?

Verse 3

Cm
I build myself up,
  Gm/B♭   B♭
And fly around in circles,
   A♭maj7
Waiting as my heart drops,
  G7
And my back begins to tingle,
  A♭6   B♭6 B♭7
Final - ly could this be it?

Chorus 2

A♭maj7
Or should I give up,
Gm Cm   Fm7   A♭
  Or should I just keep chasing pavements?
A♭6   Gm7   G7
Even if it leads no - where?
   A♭maj7   Gm
Or would it be a waste,
Cm Fm7   A♭   A♭6   G7
Even if I knew my place, should I leave it there?

cont.

A♭maj7
Should I give up,

  Gm   Cm   Fm7   A♭
   Or should I just keep chasing pavements?

A♭6   Gm7   E♭
Even if it leads nowhere? Yeah.

Chorus 3

A♭
Should I give up,

           Gm
Or should I just keep chasing pavements?

   A♭6   B♭7
Even if it leads no - where?

         A♭
Or would it be a waste,

       G7
Even if I knew my place,

        F7
Should I leave it there?

   B♭7sus4
Should I give up,

       A♭maj7   Gm Cm   Fm7
Or should I just keep on   chasing   pavements?

A♭   Gm7   Cm   Fm7   A♭ A♭6 B♭
   Should I just keep on   chasing   pavements?   Oh.

Chorus 4

A♭maj7
Should I give up,

  Gm   Cm   Fm7   A♭
   Or should I just keep chasing pavements?

A♭6   Gm7   G7
Even if it leads nowhere?

    A♭maj7   Gm
Or would it be a waste,

Cm Fm7   A♭   A♭6   G7
Even if I knew my place, should I leave it there?

A♭maj7
Should I give up,

  Gm   Cm   Fm7   A♭
   Or should I just keep chasing pavements?

A♭6   Gm7   E♭
Even if it leads nowhere?___

Charmer

Words & Music by
Caleb Followill, Nathan Followill, Jared Followill & Matthew Followill

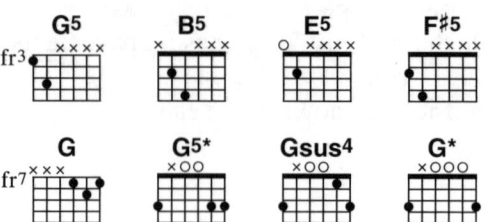

Intro ‖: G5   B5 | E5   F♯5   :‖ *play 6 times*

Verse 1
        G5   B5   E5   F♯5   G5 B5 E5
Whoa!   She's such a charmer, oh no.
F♯5   G5   B5   E5   F♯5   G5 B5 E5
  Whoa!   She's such a charmer, oh no.

Chorus 1
F♯5   G5   B5   E5   F♯5
  Whoa!   She's always looking at me.
G5   B5   E5   F♯5
Whoa!   She's always looking at me.
G5   B5   E5   F♯5   G5 B5 E5
Whoa!   She's such a charmer oh no,
F♯5
Oh no.

Link 1 ‖: G5   B5 | E5   F♯5   :‖

Verse 2
       G5   B5   E5   F♯5 G5 B5 E5
Whoa!   She stole my karma, oh no.
F♯5 G5 B5 E5 F♯5 G5 B5 E5
  Sold   it to the farmer, oh no.

© Copyright 2007 Martha Street Music/Followill Music/Songs Of Combustion Music/
McFearless Music/Coffee Tea Or Me Publishing.
Bug Music Limited (45%)/P & P Songs Limited (55%).
All Rights Reserved. International Copyright Secured.

Chorus 2

    F#5   G5   B5   E5   F#5
Whoa!   She's always looking at me.
        G5   B5   E5   F#5
Whoa!   She's always looking at me.
        G5   B5   E5   F#5   G5 B5 E5
Whoa!   She's such a charmer oh no,
F#5
Oh no.

Interlude 1

| G | G | |

|: G5   B5 | E5   F#5 :| *play 4 times*

Verse 2

      G5 B5   E5   F#5   G5 B5 E5
Born in West Vir - ginia, oh no.
F#5   G5 B5   E5   F#5 G5 B5 E5
  Mar - ried, to the preacher, oh no.

Chorus 3

    F#5   G5   B5   E5   F#5
Whoa!   She's always looking at me.
        G5   B5   E5   F#5
Whoa!   She's always looking at me.
        G5   B5   E5   F#5   G5 B5 E5
Whoa!   She's such a charmer oh no,
F#5   G5
Oh no.

Interlude 2

| (G) | (G) | |

| (G) | |

|: (G) | (G) G5* Gsus4 G* :| *play 4 times*

|: G5   B5 | E5   F#5 :| *play 4 times*

| G | G | |

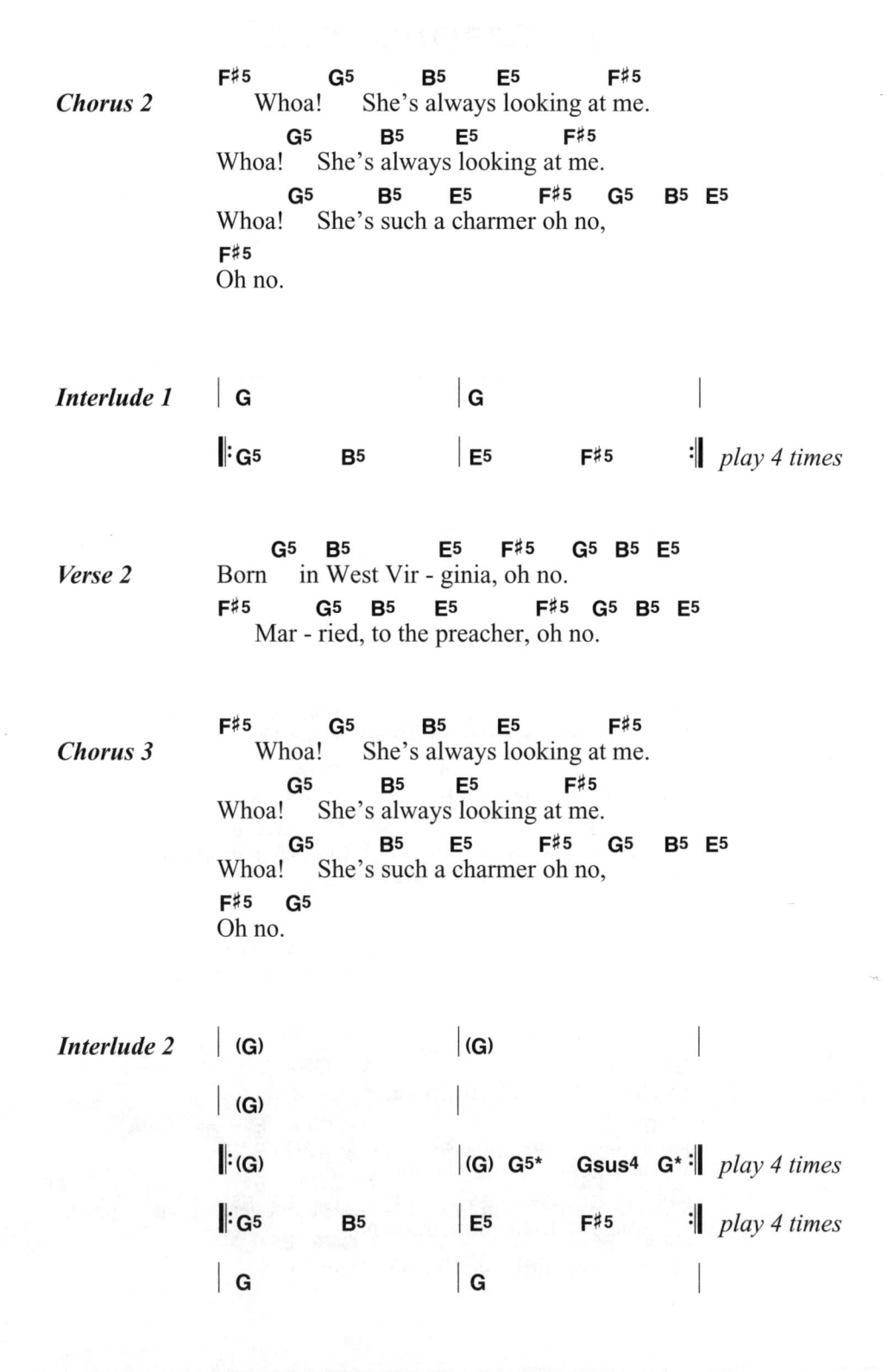

Chorus 4   As Chorus 3.

23

Dig, Lazarus, Dig!!!

Words & Music by
Nick Cave

E5   A5   G5/A   B5   C   G   D

Intro

‖: E5   A5 G5/A | E5   A5 G5/A |
| E5   A5 G5/A | B5   :‖

Chorus 1

      E5   A5   G5/A
‖: Dig yourself, Laza - rus, :‖ *play 3 times*
B5   (E5)
Dig yourself back in that hole.
                (Larry…)

Verse 1

E5   A5   G5/A E5   A5 G5/A
Larry made his nest up in the au - tumn branches,
E5   A5   G5/A E5   A5 G5/A
Built from nothing but high hopes and thin air.
     E5   A5   G5/A E5
He col - lected up some ba - by - bla - sted mothers,
             A5 G5/A
They took their chances,
        E5   A5 G5/A E5 A5
And for a while they lived quite hap - pily up there.
G5/A E5   A5
He   came from New York cit - y, man,
G5/A E5   A5 G5/A
But he couldn't take the pace,
    E5   A5 G5/A E5 A5 G5/A
He thought it was like dog eat dog world.
      E5   A5 G5/A E5   A5
Then he went to San Francis - co, spent a year in outer space,
G5/A E5   A5   G5/A E5 A5
With a sweet little San Francis - can girl.

© Copyright 2008 Mute Song.
All Rights Reserved. International Copyright Secured.

Bridge 1

    G5/A E5   A5
I can hear my mother wailing,

    G5/A   E5   A5 G5/A E5   A5   G5/A
And a whole lot of scrap - ing of   chairs,

   E5 A5 G5/A   C
       I   don't know what it is,

                   G   D   (E5)
But there's definately something going on up - stairs.
                                                    (Dig…)

Chorus 2

   E5   A5   G5/A
‖: Dig yourself, Laza - rus, :‖ *play 3 times*

B5   E5   A5 G5/A
Dig yourself back in that hole.

E5   A5 G5/A E5 A5 G5/A
  I want you to   dig,

B5
  I want you to dig.

Verse 2

      E5   A5
Well yeah, New York City,

G5/A   E5
He had to get out of there,

A5   G5/A   E5   A5 G5/A
And San Fran - sisco, well I don't know.

E5   A5   G5/A E5
   And then to L.A.,   where he   spent about a day,

A5   G5/A   E5   A5
He thought even the pale sky stars,

G5/A E5   A5   G5/A
Were smart enough to keep well away from L.A.

Link 1 | E5   A5 G5/A |

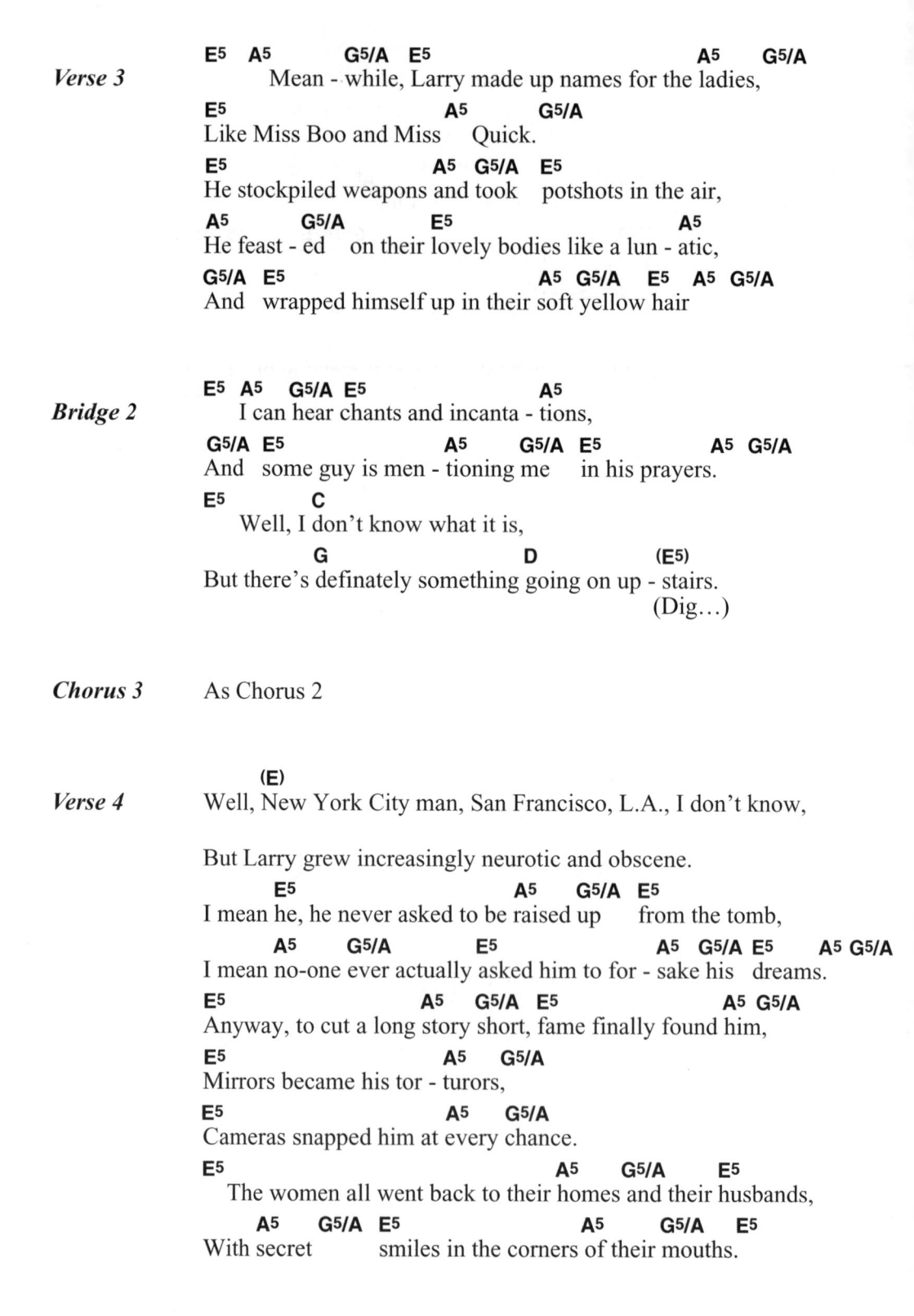

Verse 3

E5   A5   G5/A E5   A5   G5/A
     Mean - while, Larry made up names for the ladies,
E5   A5   G5/A
Like Miss Boo and Miss   Quick.
E5   A5 G5/A E5
He stockpiled weapons and took   potshots in the air,
A5   G5/A   E5   A5
He feast - ed   on their lovely bodies like a lun - atic,
G5/A E5   A5 G5/A E5   A5 G5/A
And   wrapped himself up in their soft yellow hair

Bridge 2

E5 A5   G5/A E5   A5
     I can hear chants and incanta - tions,
G5/A E5   A5   G5/A E5   A5 G5/A
And   some guy is men - tioning me   in his prayers.
E5   C
     Well, I don't know what it is,
            G   D   (E5)
But there's definately something going on up - stairs.
                                         (Dig…)

Chorus 3   As Chorus 2

Verse 4
          (E)
Well, New York City man, San Francisco, L.A., I don't know,

But Larry grew increasingly neurotic and obscene.
          E5   A5   G5/A E5
I mean he, he never asked to be raised up   from the tomb,
        A5   G5/A   E5   A5   G5/A E5   A5 G5/A
I mean no-one ever actually asked him to for - sake his   dreams.
E5   A5   G5/A E5   A5 G5/A
Anyway, to cut a long story short, fame finally found him,
E5   A5   G5/A
Mirrors became his tor - turors,
E5   A5   G5/A
Cameras snapped him at every chance.
E5   A5   G5/A   E5
   The women all went back to their homes and their husbands,
       A5   G5/A E5   A5   G5/A   E5
With secret   smiles in the corners of their mouths.

Verse 5

```
     A5  G5/A     E5              A5      G5/A
         He ended up like so many of them do;
 E5                       A5   G5/A E5
    Back on the streets of New York City,
             A5   G5/A  E5          A5     G5/A
 In a soup queue,      a dope fiend, a slave,
 E5         A5 G5/A       E5        A5           G5/A
   Then pris - on,     then the madhouse, then the grave.
 E5 A5 G5/A E5    A5
    Ah, poor   Larry,
 G5/A E5                       A5      G5/A
 But   what do we really know of the dead,
 E5          A5    G5/A E5   A5 G5/A
    And who ac - tual - ly    cares?
```

Bridge 3

```
       E5 A5   G5/A  C
          Well, I    don't know what it is,
                G             D          (E5)
 But there's definately something going on up - stairs.
                                              (Dig…)
```

Chorus 4

```
       E5           A5     G5/A
 ‖: Dig yourself, Laza - rus,
    E5           A5     G5/A
    Dig yourself, Laza - rus,
    E5           A5     G5/A
    Dig yourself, Laza - rus,
    B5
    Dig yourself back in that hole. :‖ play 3 times
    E5           A5     G5/A
    Dig yourself, Laza - rus,
    E5           A5     G5/A
    Dig yourself, Laza - rus,
    E5           A5     G5/A
    Dig yourself, Laza - rus,
    B5                      E5
    Dig yourself back in that hole.
```

Floods

Words & Music by
Charles Simpson, Alexander Westaway, Daniel Haigh & Omar Abidi

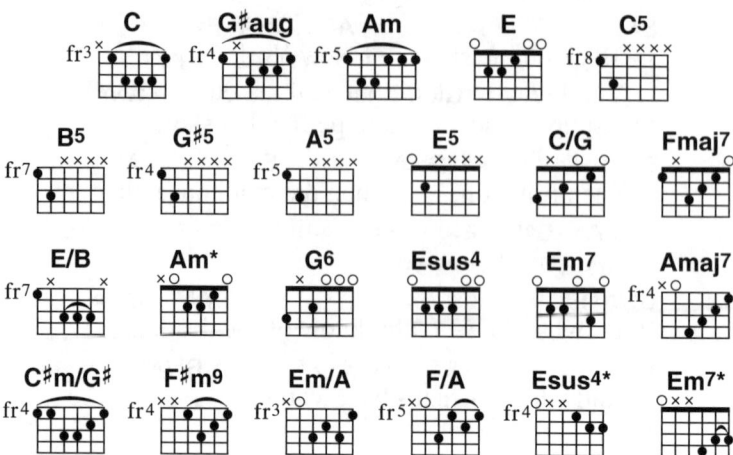

To match recording tune all strings down a semitone

Intro | C | G♯aug |
            | Am | E |
            | C5   B5 | G♯5 |
            | A5 | E5 |

Verse 1
      Am   G♯aug
You can all pretend,_____
                   C/G
That you don't know enough,
             Fmaj7
Enough to make sense.
Am   E/B
All this will be gone,
            C
And you can sink beneath,
              Fmaj7
The rapture we've spawned.
Am*   G6   Fmaj7 Esus4 Em7
What have we be - come?

© Copyright 2007 Notting Hill Music (UK) Limited.
All Rights Reserved. International Copyright Secured.

Chorus 1

```
        C5                        B5           G♯5
   You know we don't have all the en - tire world,
        A5              E5
   To make the floods seem still,
        C5                        B5           G♯5
   You know we don't have all the en - tire world,
        A5            E5
   So make the most of this.
```

Verse 2

```
   Am              G♯aug
   Blind will bleed the blind,
         C/G                      Fmaj7
   When the only thing to see is their lies,
         Am              E/B
   Let not the sun go down,
          C                      Fmaj7
   On the wrath of this inconvenient truth.
   Am*    G6     Fmaj7  Esus4  Em7
   What have we be - come?
```

Chorus 2   As Chorus 1

Interlude

| Amaj7 | C♯m/G♯ | |
| Amaj7 | F♯m9 | |

Bridge

```
           Amaj7      C♯m/G♯         Amaj7   C
   Just smile like the idiots you are and swim.
```

Chorus 3   As Chorus 1

Outro

| Am | Em/A | |
| F/A | Esus4* Em7* | ||

29

Dog House Boogie

Words & Music by
Steve Wold

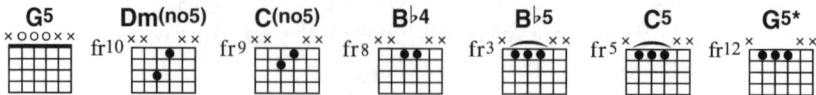

Tuning: D, G, D, G, B, D

Intro
w/slide
throughout

        G5 Dm(no5) G5   C(no5)
(vocal ad lib)…

G5   Bb4 | G5 | G5 | G5 | G5 ||
…We're gonna do the doghouse boogie.

Verse 1

  (G5)   Bb5
    All my life I've been in the doghouse,
G5   Bb5
   I guess that's just where I belong.
G5   Bb5 G5
   That's just the way the dice rolled.
      C5 Bb5   G5
So do the doghouse song.

We're gonna get personal now.

Verse 2

G5   Bb5
   You hate the kind of blues you have on one day,
G5   Bb5
   You have it your whole life long.
G5   Bb5 G5
   You got to be a professional,
C5   Bb5   G5
   To sing the doghouse song.

© Copyright 2006 Steve Wold.
All Rights Reserved. International Copyright Secured.

Chorus 1

    G5   C5   B♭5 G5
A-whoo, yeah, yeah, yeah.
G5   C5   B♭5 G5
A-whoo, yeah, yeah, yeah.
G5   C5   B♭5 G5
A-whoo, yeah, yeah, yeah.
C5   B♭5   G5* | G5* |
Sing the doghouse song.
            B♭5 C5 B♭5 G5 B♭5 C5 B♭5 G5
The dog - house,
            B♭5 C5 B♭5 G5 B♭5 C5 B♭5 G5
The dog - house,
            B♭5 C5 B♭5 G5 B♭5 C5 B♭5 G5
The dog - house,
C5   B♭5   G5
Do the doghouse song.

Verse 3

(G5)
I'm gonna tell you my story.
                                       B♭5 G5
My mum and dad broke up when I was four years old,

When I was seven, she went and got herself another man,
      B♭5   G5
It was hell   y'all.
                                  B♭5 G5
I left home when I was fourteen years of age,
                       B♭5 G5
I figured I'd do better on my own.

Then followed a number of years,
               B♭5 G5
Of bumming around and liv - ing kind of hand and mouth,
                     B♭5 G5
Sometimes getting locked up   and such,
                               B♭5 G5
And sometimes just going cold and hun - gry.
        B♭5 G5
I didn't have me no real school education,
                                B♭5 G5
So what in the hell was I gonna be able to   do?

cont. But I always did pick up the guitar
B♭5 G5
I used to put the hat out for spare change,
   B♭5 G5
But I'm making this here record for y'all,
                    B♭5 G5
And I'm still trying to get your spare change.

I don't know why it went wrong,
      B♭5 G5
It ain't bad now,   and I just keep playing my
           B♭5 G5 C5   **B♭5**   **G5**
Doghouse mu - sic,   sing the doghouse song.

Chorus 2
G5   **C5   B♭5   G5**
   A-whoo, a-whoo, yeah, yeah, yeah.
G5   **C5   B♭5   G5**
   A-whoo, a-whoo, yeah, yeah, yeah.
G5   **C5   B♭5   G5**
   A-whoo, a-whoo, yeah, yeah, yeah.
C5   B♭5   G5* | G5* |
Sing the doghouse song,
       B♭5 C5 B♭5 G5 B♭5 C5 B♭5 G5
Dog - house,
       B♭5 C5 B♭5 G5 B♭5 C5 B♭5 G5
Dog - house,
       B♭5 C5 B♭5 G5 B♭5 C5 B♭5 G5
Dog - house,
C5   B♭5   G5* | G5* |
Sing the doghouse song.
       B♭5 C5 B♭5 G5 B♭5 C5 B♭5 G5
Dog - house,
       B♭5 C5 B♭5 G5 B♭5 C5 B♭5 G5
Dog - house,
       B♭5 C5 B♭5 G5 B♭5 C5 B♭5 G5
Dog - house.

Outro
       C5   B♭5   G5   C5   B♭5   G5
𝄆 Sing the doghouse song, sing the dog - house song,
       C5   B♭5   G5*   C5   B♭5   G5*
Sing the doghouse song, sing the dog - house song. 𝄇
                           Repeat to fade w/slide ad lib.

Folding Stars

Words & Music by
Simon Neil

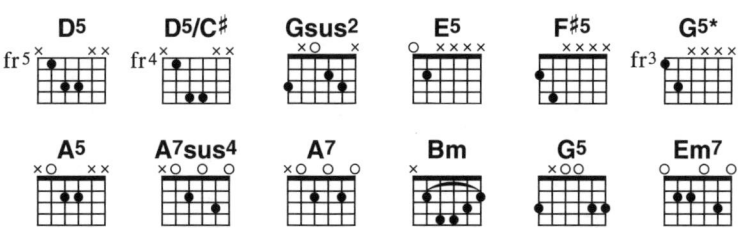

Intro | (D5) | (D5) |
  |: D5/C♯   D5   Gsus2| Gsus2   :| *play 4 times*

Verse 1
                D5/C♯   D5   Gsus2
        Take a long hard look at your - self,
        D5/C♯   D5   Gsus2
        How did you end up here?
                D5/C♯   D5   Gsus2
        The blood drips like red in - verted balloons,

Bridge 1
                D5/C♯   D5   Gsus2
        To - morrow is a promise to no-one.
                E5   F♯5   G5*   A5
        If you want, follow me and I'll lead you inside,
                 E5   F♯5   G5*   A5
        You don't have to   run and hide.

Chorus 1
          D5   A7sus4   A7   Bm
        Elea - nor,   Elea - nor,
                        G5   Em7
        I would do anything for another minute with you,
                      D5   A5
        'Cause it's not getting easier, it's not getting easier.

© 2006 Good Soldier Songs Limited.
Universal Music Publishing Limited.
All rights in Germany administered by Universal Music Publ. GmbH.
All Rights Reserved. International Copyright Secured.

Link   ‖: D5/C♯   D5   Gsus2 Gsus2   :‖

Verse 2
    D5/C♯   D5   Gsus2
   In a bedroom with no windows or doors,
   D5/C♯   D5   Gsus2
   All the happy people are crying.
     D5/C♯   D5   Gsus2
   You can't hold a gaze for a second or two,
    D5/C♯   D5 Gsus2
   It always ends in total darkness.

Bridge 2 As Bridge 1

Chorus 2
   D5 A7sus4 A7 Bm
   Elea - nor, Elea - nor,
     G5   Em7
   I would do anything for another minute with you,
     D5   A5
   'Cause it's not getting easier, it's not getting easier.
     D5   A7sus4 A7 Bm
   You will be folding stars, Elea - nor,
     G5   Em7
   You can't ever understand, (you can't ever understand,)
     D5   A5
   It's not getting easier, it's not getting easier.

Interlude 1 ‖: D5/C♯ D5 Gsus2 Gsus2   :‖ *play 4 times*

Bridge 3

```
            E5           F#5              G5*         A5
         It ends in a place    with no love,  only hate,
            E5         F#5        G5*   A5
         And a mirror re - flecting the truth.
            E5                F#5              G5*       A5
         In your eyes, in your face   you can't wash   it a - way,
                       E5    F#5    G5*   A5
         From your cold,  cold    heart._____
```

Chorus 3

```
            D5     A7sus4  A7    Bm
         Elea - nor,    Elea - nor,
                  G5                    Em7
         I would do anything for another minute with you,
                D5                   A5
         'Cause it's not getting easier, it's not getting easier.
               D5        A7sus4  A7    Bm
         You will be folding stars,   Elea - nor,
               G5                      Em7
         You can't ever understand, (you can't ever understand,)
               D5                 A5
         It's not getting easier, it's not getting easier.
```

Interlude 2   ‖: D5/C#   D5   Gsus2│ Gsus2   :‖

Outro

```
              D5/C#       D5      Gsus2
         It's not getting easier,      not getting easier,
              D5/C#          D5      Gsus2   D5
         I hope that you're folding stars.
```

Gilt Complex

Words & Music by
Adele Bethel, Ailidh Lennon, David Gow & Scott Paterson

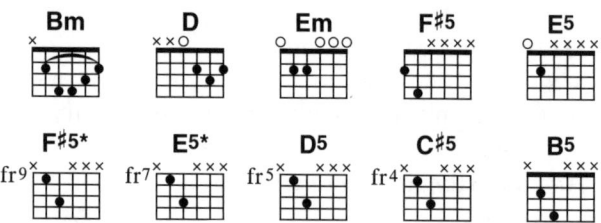

Intro ‖: Bm | Bm | |
| Bm | Bm :‖ *play 4 times*

Verse 1
       Bm
She has a gilt complex, break her neck,

And now she's run, run, running right over the edge.

Had a gilt complex, poison pen,

She's signing her name and she's forgetting her friends.

Had a gilt complex, break her neck,
      D   Bm
Now she worry, worry, worries for the good of her wealth.

This gilt complex, useless effect,
      D   Bm
Now she suffer, suffer, suffers, de - stroying her health.

Link 1 ‖: Bm | Bm | |
| Bm | Bm :‖

© Copyright 2007 Bug Music Limited (PRS).
All Rights Reserved. International Copyright Secured.

Verse 2

       Bm
He has a gilt complex, break his neck,

Now he's run, run, running right over the edge.

Had a gilt complex, poison pen,

Signing his name, forgetting his friends.

Had a gilt complex, break his neck,
  D   **Bm**
Now he worry, worry, worries for the good of his wealth.

This gilt complex, useless effect,
  D   **Bm**
Now he suffer, suffer, suffers, de - stroying himself.

Chorus 2

Em
All you see is all you'll get,
                        Bm
He's trying to buy some kind of medal.
Em
He's not sure of all he has but,
          F♯5   **E5**
Avarice is all that he's made of,___
  F♯5* **E5*** **D5**   **C♯5** **B5**
And ev - 'ry - bod - y   knows.

Link 2   As Link 1

Verse 3   As Verse 1

Chorus 3

    Em
All you see is all you'll get,

                                 Bm
She's trying to buy some kind of medal.

Em
She's not sure of all she has but,

                    F♯5   **E5**
Avarice is all that she's made of,___

   F♯5* E5* D5   **C♯5 B5**
And ev - 'ry - bod - y   knows.

Link 3   As Link 1

Interlude

  Bm
Ooh.

    Bm
$\|:$ Why-ooh-ooh, why-ooh-ooh,

Why-ooh-ooh, why-ooh-ooh. $:\|$

Chorus 4

Em
What you see is what you'll get,

                                Bm
The star, you see is just made of metal.

Em
He's not sure of all he has,

                        F♯5   **E5**
But avarice is all that he's made of,___

   F♯5* E5* D5   **C♯5 B5**
And ev - 'ry - bod - y   knows.

Outro | **Bm** | **Bm** |

                | **Bm** | **Bm**   ‖

Great DJ

Words & Music by
Katie White & Jules De Martino

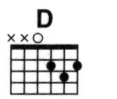

D Dadd♭6 Am7

Intro ‖: D | Dadd♭6 :‖ *play 8 times*

Verse 1
D
Fed up with your indigestion,

Swallow words one by one.

Your folks got high at a quarter to five,

Don't you feel you're growing up undone?
            Dadd♭6
Nothing but the local D.J.
  D   Dadd♭6
He said he had some songs to play.
 D   Dadd♭6
What went down from this fooling around,
       D
Gave hope and a brand new day.

© Copyright 2007 Sony/ATV Music Publishing (UK) Limited (50%)/Copyright Control (50%).
All Rights Reserved. International Copyright Secured.

Chorus 1

     D   **Am7**
Imagine all the girls, ah-ah, ah, ah, ah-ah, ah-ah,
   D   **Am7**
And the boys, ah-ah, ah, ah, ah-ah, ah-ah,
   D   **Am7**
And the strings, eeh-eeh, eeh, eeh, eeh-eeh, eeh-eeh,
   D   **Am7**
And the drums, the drums, the drums, the drums.
  D
‖: The drums, the drums. :‖ *play 4 times*

Oh.

Link   ‖: **D** | **Dadd♭6**   :‖

Verse 2

  D   **Dadd♭6**
Nothing was the same a - gain,
  D   **Dadd♭6**
All about where and when.
  D   **Dadd♭6**
Blowing our minds in a life unkind,
   D   **Dadd♭6**
You gotta love the B.P.M.
  D   **Dadd♭6**
When his work was all but done,
   D   **Dadd♭6**
Remembering how this be - gun.
   D   **Dadd♭6**
We wore his love like a hand in a glove,
     D
There's a future, plays it all night long.

Chorus 2

                    D   **Am7**
Nothing but the girls, ah-ah, ah, ah, ah-ah, ah-ah,
      D   **Am7**
And the boys, ah-ah, ah, ah, ah-ah, ah-ah,
      D   **Am7**
And the strings, eeh-eeh, eeh, eeh, eeh-eeh, eeh-eeh,
      D   **Am7**
And the drums, the drums, the drums, the drums.
       D   **Am7**
‖: The drums, the drums, the drums, the drums. :‖ *play 4 times*

Interlude   ‖: **D** | **Am7**   :‖ *play 4 times*

Chorus 3

              D   **Am7**
Imagine all the girls, ah-ah, ah, ah, ah-ah, ah-ah,
      D   **Am7**
And the boys, ah-ah, ah, ah, ah-ah, ah-ah,
      D   **Am7**
And the strings, eeh-eeh, eeh, eeh, eeh-eeh, eeh-eeh,
      D   **Am7**
And the drums, ah-ah, ah, ah, ah-ah, ah-oh.
      D   **Am7**
All the girls, ah-ah, ah, ah, ah-ah, ah-ah,
D   **Am7**
And the boys, ah-ah, ah, ah, ah-ah, ah-ah,
D   **Am7**
And the strings, eeh-eeh, eeh, eeh, eeh-eeh, eeh-eeh,
      D   **Am7**
And the drums, the drums, the drums, the drums.

I'm A Realist

**Words & Music by
Gary Jarman, Ross Jarman & Ryan Jarman**

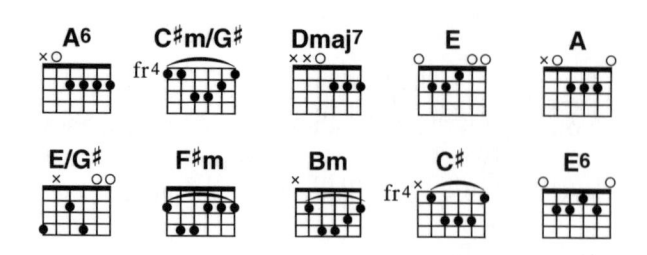

Intro

|: A6 | C♯m/G♯ |

| Dmaj7 | E   :|

Verse 1

    A   E/G♯ F♯m
I'm a realist,   I'm a romantic,
  Bm
I'm an indecisive, I'm an indecisive,
           E
Piece of shit.
   A   E/G♯ F♯m
I'm a realist,   I'm a romantic,
  Bm
I am indecisive, I am indecisive,
            E
And that's about it.

Chorus 1

          A6   C♯m/G♯
And you dream that's the same thing,
        Dmaj7
That's the same life you lead.
E   A6
 I don't agree and so you drink,
      C♯m/G♯
Don't wanna think,
              Dmaj7   E   A6
That's 'cause your mind is   already made up.

© Copyright 2007 Chrysalis Music Limited.
All Rights Reserved. International Copyright Secured.

Verse 2

```
        A         E/G♯  F♯m
   I'm a realist,     I'm a romantic,
        Bm
I'm an indecisive, I'm an indecisive,
              E
Piece of shit.
    A       E/G♯    F♯m
  I admit it,    I'm up to my old tricks,
        Bm
Did you see her eyes, oh no I tried,
                        E
She looked surprised.
```

Chorus 2

```
             A6                 C♯m/G♯
    And you dream that's the same thing,
             Dmaj7
That's the same life you lead.
E                      A6
  I don't agree and so you drink,
         C♯m/G♯
Don't wanna think,
              Dmaj7   E
That's 'cause your mind is   already made up.
         A6                 C♯m/G♯
And you dream that's the same thing,
             Dmaj7
That's the same life you lead.
E                      A6
  I don't agree and so you drink,
         C♯m/G♯
Don't wanna think,
              Dmaj7   E
That's 'cause your mind is   already made up.
```

Bridge
   A   **C♯**
I know that it's only a matter of time,

Before you know it I'll be leaving town.
Bm   **E6**   **E**
See it in my eyes, that no-one will do,
E6   **E**
No-one will ever do.
A   **C♯**
I know that it's only a matter of time,

Before you know it I'll be leaving town.
Bm   **E6**   **E**
Seen it in your eyes, no-one will do,
E6   **E**   **(A6)**
No-one will ever do for you.

Interlude ‖: **A6** | **C♯m/G♯** |
      (you.)
      | **Dmaj7** | **E**   :‖

Outro
    A6
‖: La-la-la, la-la-la, la-la,
C♯m/G♯
La-la-la, la-la-la, la-la,
Dmaj7
La-la-la, la-la-la, la-la,
E
La-la-la, whoa-oh. :‖

  | **A6**   ‖

I'm Like A Lawyer With The Way I'm Always Trying To Get You Off (Me & You)

Words & Music by
Peter Wentz, Andrew Hurley, Joseph Trohman & Patrick Stumph

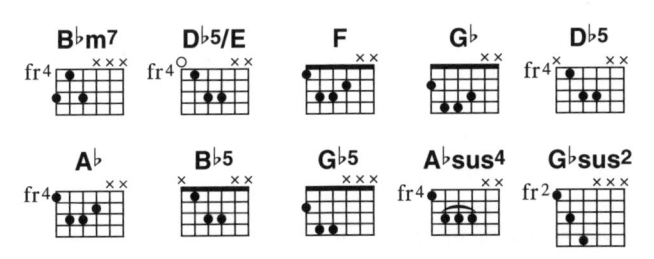

B♭m7	D♭5/E	F	G♭	D♭5
A♭	B♭5	G♭5	A♭sus4	G♭sus2

Verse 1

  B♭m7   D♭5/E B♭m7   D♭5/E
Last year's wishes are this year's a - pologies,
 B♭m7   F   G♭
Every last time I come home,
    B♭m7   D♭5   B♭m7   D♭5
I take my last chance to burn a bridge or two.
   B♭m7   F
I only keep myself this sick in the head,
  G♭
'Cause I know how the words get you.

Pre-chorus 1

  F   B♭m7
We're the new face of failure,
 F   B♭m7
Prettier and younger but not any better off,
 A♭   D♭5 G♭5 F
Bulletproof loneli - ness at best, at best.

Chorus 1

 A♭ D♭5   B♭5
Me and you, setting in a honeymoon,
  G♭
If I woke up next to you,

If I woke up next to you.
    B♭5   D♭5
Me and you, setting in a honeymoon,
  G♭5
If I woke up next to you,
 A♭5
If I woke up next to you.

© Copyright 2007 Sony/ATV Music Publishing (UK) Limited.
All Rights Reserved. International Copyright Secured.

Verse 2

    B♭m7   D♭5
Col - lect the bad habits,
   B♭m7   D♭5
That you couldn't bear to keep,
B♭m7   F G♭
Out of the woods, but I love,
    B♭m7   D♭5
A tree, I used to lay be - neath.
     B♭m7   D♭5
Kissed teeth stained red,
   B♭m7 F
From a sour bottle baby girl,
  G♭
With eyes the size of baby worlds.

Pre-chorus 2

   F   B♭m7
We're the new face of failure,
   F   B♭m7
Prettier and younger but not any better off,
A♭   D♭5 G♭5 F
Bulletproof loneli - ness at best, at best.

Chorus 2

 A♭ D♭5   B♭5
Me and you, setting in a honeymoon,
  G♭
If I woke up next to you,

If I woke up next to you.
   B♭5   D♭5
Me and you, setting in a honeymoon,
  G♭5
If I woke up next to you,

If I woke up next to you.
   D♭5   B♭5
Me and you, setting in a honeymoon,
  G♭
If I woke up next to you,

If I woke up next to you.
   B♭5   D♭5
Me and you, setting in a honeymoon,
  G♭5
If I woke up next to you,
  A♭5
If I woke up next to you.

Bridge

    B♭5   **G♭5**
And the best way to make it through,
 D♭5   **F5**
With hearts and wrists in - tact,
 B♭5 **G♭5**   **A♭sus4** **A♭**
Is to realise two out of three ain't bad, ain't bad.

Chorus 3

 D♭5
Me and you, setting in a honeymoon,
 G♭
If I woke up next to you,

If I woke up next to you.
 B♭5 **D♭5**
Me and you, honeymoon,
G♭5
Setting in a honeymoon.
 D♭5   **B♭5**
Me and you, setting in a honeymoon,
 G♭
If I woke up next to you,

If I woke up next to you.
 B♭5   **D♭5**
Me and you, setting in a honeymoon,
 G♭   **G♭sus2**
If I woke up next to you, honeymoon.

Indian Summer

Words & Music by
James Dean Bradfield, Nicky Wire & Sean Moore

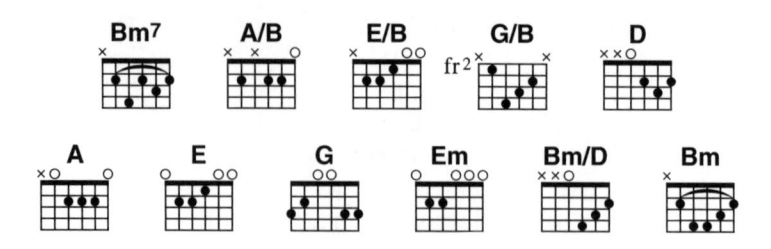

Intro   ‖: Bm7 | A/B | |
            | E/B | G/B   :‖

Verse 1
```
        D                    A
If God persists, persists in saying yes,
      E                        G
I guess we'll have, we'll have to test ourselves.
      D                               A
Maybe the summer will come and clear our minds,
        E                         G
And find the impulse to love the sunshine.
```

Pre-chorus 1
```
  Em D  G
   I guess we'll have to test,
  Bm E    G
   Un - til there's nothing left.
  Em D  G
   We said the truth was fixed,
  Bm E    G
   It's lost without a trace.
```

© Copyright 2007 Sony/ATV Music Publishing (UK) Limited.
All Rights Reserved. International Copyright Secured.

Chorus 1

          Bm7
This crime is e - ternity,
               A/B
When time lost its certainty,
     E/B   **G/B**
The Indian summer.

Verse 2

D   **A**
Maybe this time, we'll kiss and we'll not shake hands.
E   **G**
Indian Summer, still hurt and broken.
   D   **A**
And leave all this materi -al belief,
    E   **G**
Re - member the reasons, the reasons that made us be.

Pre-chorus 2

Em D G
    I guess we'll have to test,
Bm E   **G**
    What's darker than ourselves.
Em D   **G**
    We said the truth was fixed,
Bm E   **G**
    It's lost without a trace.

Chorus 2

          Bm7
This crime is e - ternity,
               A/B
When time lost its certainty,
     E/B   **G/B**
The Indian summer.
       Bm7   **A/B**
The Indian summer, the Indian summer,
     E/B   **G/B**
The Indian summer.

Interlude | D | A |
             | Em | G |
             | D | A |
             | E | G   ‖

Pre-chorus 3
    Em D   G
        I guess we'll have to test,
    Bm E   G
        Un - til there's nothing left.
    Em D   G
        We said the truth was fixed,
    Bm E   G
        It's lost without a trace.

Link | Bm7 | A/B |
          | E/B | G/B |

Chorus 3
            Bm7
    This crime is eternity,
               A/B
    When time lost its certainty,
          E/B   G/B
    The Indian summer.
          Bm7   A/B
    The Indian summer, the Indian summer,
          E/B   G/B
    The Indian summer.

Outro | Bm7 | A/B |
           | E/B | G/B |
           | Bm/D | Bm   ‖

It Means Nothing

**Words & Music by
Kelly Jones**

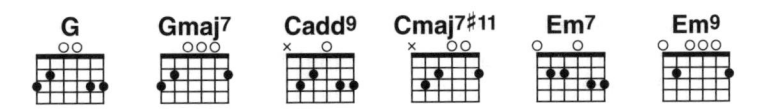

G   Gmaj7   Cadd9   Cmaj7#11   Em7   Em9

Capo 2nd fret

Intro | G   Gmaj7 | G   Gmaj7 |

| Cadd9   Cmaj7#11 | Cadd9   Cmaj7#11 |

Verse 1

      G   Gmaj7
Did we lose ourselves a - gain?
     G   Gmaj7
Do we take in what's been said?
  Cadd9   Cmaj7#11
Do we take the time to be,
   Cadd9   Cmaj7#11
All the things we said we'd be?
   G   Gmaj7
And we bury heads in sand,
   G   Gmaj7
But my future's in my hands.
   Cadd9   Cmaj7#11
It means nothing,
   Cadd9   Cmaj7#11
It means nothing.

© Copyright 2007 Stereophonics Music Limited.
Universal Music Publishing Limited.
All rights in Germany administered by Universal Music Publ. GmbH.
All Rights Reserved. International Copyright Secured.

Verse 2

    G   **Gmaj7**
You can find yourself a God,
  G   **Gmaj7**
Be - lieve in which one you want,
   Cadd9
'Cause they love you all the same,
   Cadd9   **Cmaj7#11**
They just go by different names.
    G   **Gmaj7**
When we fly our flag to - day,
    G   **Gmaj7**
Are you proud or just a - shamed?
   Cadd9 **Cmaj7#11**
It means nothing,
    Cadd9 **Cmaj7#11**
It means nothing.

Chorus 1

    Em7 **Em9**   **Em7** **Em9**
It means nothing, it means nothing.
   Cadd9 **Cmaj7#11** **Cadd9** **Cmaj7#11**
It means nothing,
    Em7 **Em9**
If I haven't got you,
    Em7 **Em9**
If I haven't got you,
     Cadd9 **Cmaj7#11**
If I haven't got you,
     Cadd9 **Cmaj7#11**
If I haven't got you.

Verse 3

    G   **Gmaj7**
And the sun sits in the sky,
    G   **Gmaj7**
You're the apple of my eye.
   Cadd9   **Cmaj7#11**
If the bomb goes off a - gain,
   Cadd9   **Cmaj7#11**
In my brain or on the train,
  G   **Gmaj7**
I hope that I'm with you,
   G   **Gmaj7**
'Cause I wouldn't know what to do.
   Cadd9 **Cmaj7#11**
It means nothing,
    Cadd9 **Cmaj7#11**
It means nothing.

Chorus 2

     Em7 **Em9**   **Em7** **Em9**
It means nothing, it means nothing.
      Cadd9 **Cmaj7#11** **Cadd9** **Cmaj7#11**
It means nothing,
     Em7 **Em9**
If I haven't got you,
     Em7 **Em9**
If I haven't got you,
      Cadd9 **Cmaj7#11**
If I haven't got you,
      Cadd9 **Cmaj7#11**
If I haven't got you.

Interlude

       G **Gmaj7** **G** **Gmaj7**
If I haven't got you,_____
Cadd9 **Cmaj7#11** **Cadd9** **Cmaj7#11**
You,_____ ah,_____
Em7
Oh, ah, oh, ah.
Cadd9 **Cmaj7#11** **Cadd9** **Cmaj7#11**
Oh,_____ ah,_____
G **Gmaj7** **G** **Gmaj7**
Oh, ah, oh, ah,
Cadd9 **Cmaj7#11** **Cadd9** **Cmaj7#11**
Oh, ah, oh, ah.

Outro

      G   **Gmaj7**   **G**   **Gmaj7**
‖: It means nothing, it means nothing,
     Cadd9 **Cmaj7#11**   **Cadd9** **Cmaj7#11**
It means nothing,   it means nothing. :‖ *repeat to fade*

Just For Tonight

**Words & Music by
Jack Sails, Daniel Parkin, Mark Hayton, Samuel Ford & George Craig**

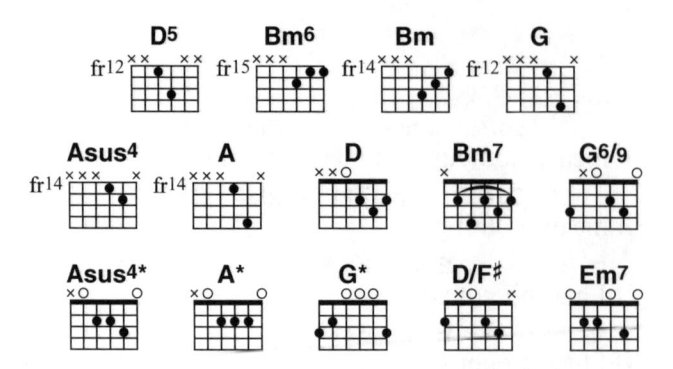

Intro ‖: D5 | D5 :‖ *play 4 times*

‖: D5 | D5 |
| Bm6 | Bm |
| G | G |
| Asus4 | A :‖

Verse 1
    D
  Way across the plains,
    Bm7
The lights spell out a code,
G6/9
  No-one knows where they take us,
    Asus4*
But we'll search till we grow old.
  D
  All the paths they lead,
    Bm7
To the single solemn place,
G6/9
  Then we'll stay for a weekend,
    Asus4*   A*
And leave without a trace.

© Copyright 2007 Chrysalis Music Limited.
All Rights Reserved. International Copyright Secured.

Chorus 1

‖:   **D5**   **Bm6**
    Just for to - night,
                    G
    Just maybe we've made it,
                Asus4
    Sing like you want this,
    A
    Sing like you want this. :‖

Interlude 1

‖: D | D |
| Bm7 | Bm7 |
| G6/9 | G6/9 |
| Asus4* | A*   :‖

Verse 2

            D
    We can take tonight,
        Bm7
    Take our time,
              G6/9
    So sing like you need this,
                Asus4* **A***
    And be who you want to.
    D
      All the paths they lead,
      Bm7
    To a little standing place,
    G6/9
      And if you stay for the weekend,
            Asus4*   **A***
    You'd leave without a trace.

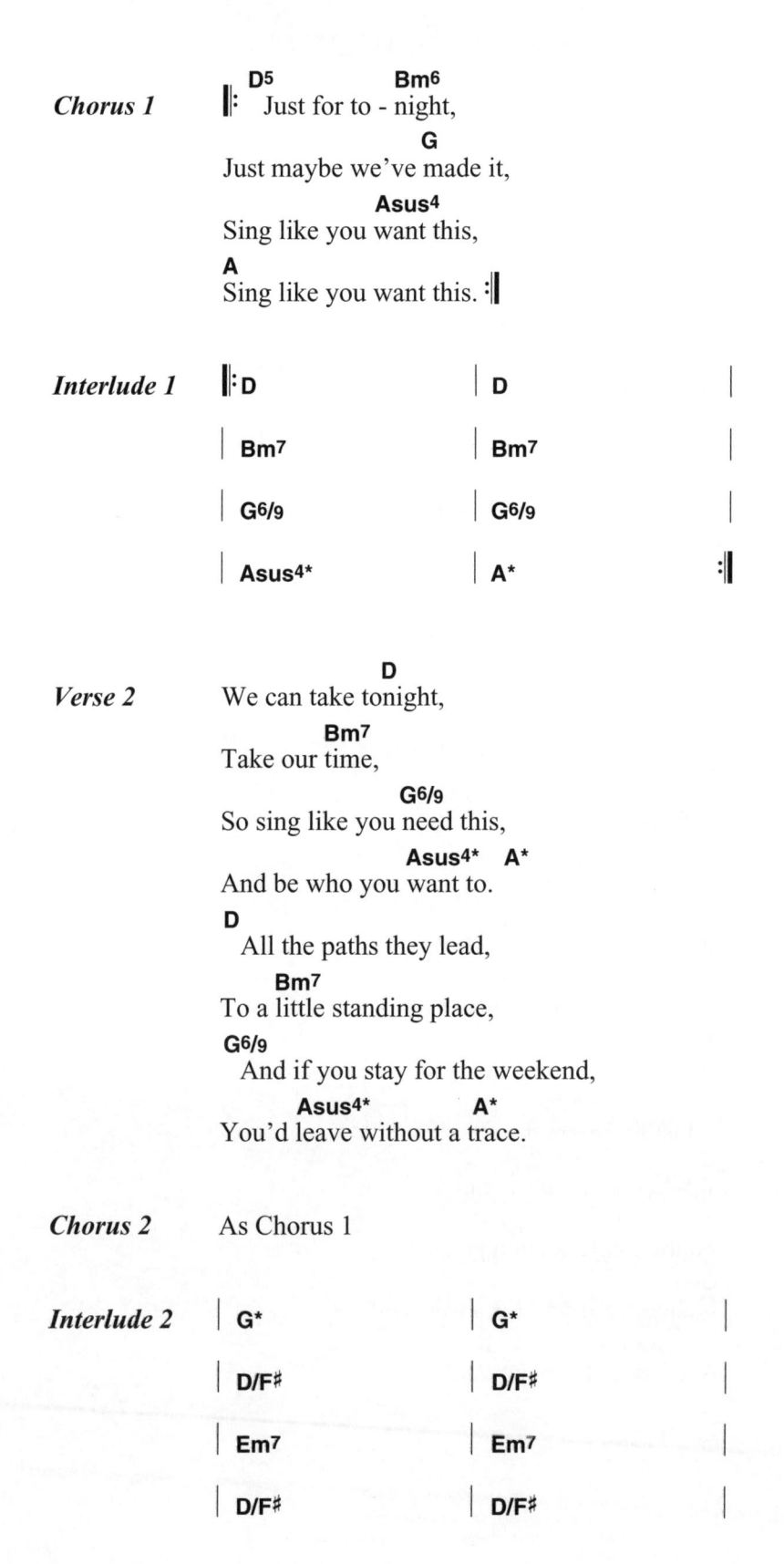

Chorus 2   As Chorus 1

Interlude 2

G*	G*
D/F♯	D/F♯
Em7	Em7
D/F♯	D/F♯

Bridge

G*
La-la, la-la, la, la-la, la,
D/F♯
La-la, la-la, la, ho-ho, ho,
Em7
La-la, la-la, la, ho-ho, ho,
A*
Ho-ho, ho.

Interlude 3

𝄆 **D**	**D**	
Bm7	**Bm7**	
G6/9	**G6/9**	
A*	**A***	𝄇

Chorus 3

      D
Just for to - night,
          Bm6 **Bm**
Just for to - night,
              G
Just maybe we've made it,
            Asus4
Sing like you want this,
A
Sing like you want this.
D   **Bm**
  Just for to - night,
              G
Just maybe we've made it,
            Asus4
Sing like you want this,
A   **D**
Sing like you want this. ⎯

The Kill

**Words & Music by
Jared Leto**

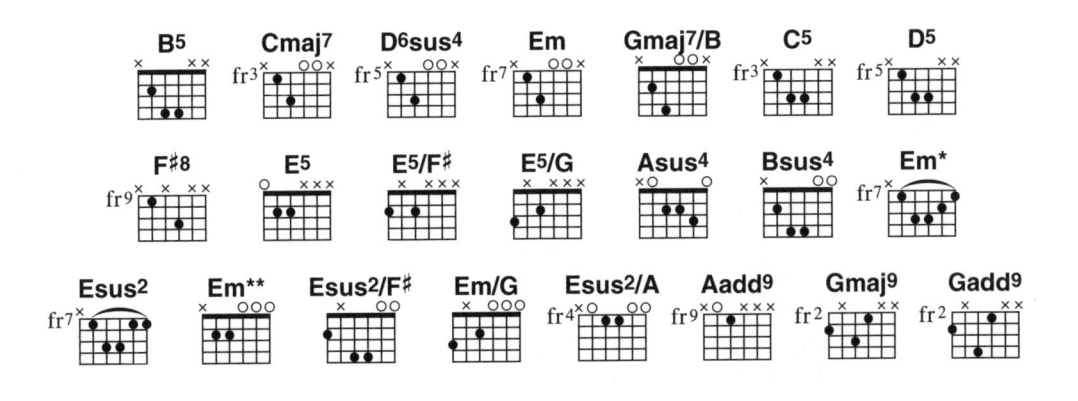

Intro | B5 ‖

Verse 1

  Cmaj7   **D6sus4**
  What if I wanted to break,
       Em
Laugh it all off in your face,
      Gmaj7/B
What would you do?
Cmaj7   **D6sus4**
  What if I fell to the floor,
       Em
Couldn't take this any - more,
      Gmaj7/B
What would you do, do, do?

Chorus 1

C5   **D5**
Come, break me down,
   F#8
Bury me, bury me,
E5 **E5/F#** **E5/G** **B5** **Bsus4**
I am finished with you.

© Copyright 2006 Zomba Music Publishers Limited.
All Rights Reserved. International Copyright Secured.

Verse 2

    Cmaj7   **D6sus4**
    What if I wanted to fight,
                     Em
Beg for the rest of my life,
                 Gmaj7/B
What would you do?
    Cmaj7
You say you wanted more,
D6sus4
What are you waiting for?
Em   **Gmaj7/B**
I'm not running from you.

Chorus 2

  C5   **D5**
Come, break me down,
     F#8
Bury me, bury me,
E5   **E5/F#**   **E5/G**
I am finished   with you.
C5   **D5**
Look in my eyes,

You're killing me, killing me,
E5   **B5**
All I wanted was you.

Bridge

  Asus4   **Bsus4**   **Em*** **Esus2**
   I tried to be someone else,
  Em   **Esus2**   **Asus4**
But nothing seemed to change,
  Bsus4   **Em**** **Esus2/F#** **Em/G** **Esus2/A**   **Cmaj7**
I know now, this is who I   really am   in - side.
        Gmaj7/B **D6sus4** **Em**
I finally found   my - self,
       Cmaj7
Fighting for a chance,
  D6sus4   **E5**
I know now, this is who I really am.

Interlude

|: **Em** **C5**
  Oh, oh.   :| *play 3 times*

| **Aadd9** | **Gmaj9**   **Gadd9** |

| **N.C.** ||

Chorus 3

C5   **D5**
Come, break me down,
        F♯8
Bury me, bury me,
E5   **E5/F♯**   **E5/G**
I am finished   with you.
C5   **D5**
Look in my eyes,

You're killing me, killing me,
E5   **B5**
All I wanted was you.

Outro

Cmaj7   **D6sus4**
Come, break me down,
          Em   **B5**
Break me down, break me down.
Cmaj7   **D6sus4**
    What if I wanted to break?

What are you waiting for?
Em   **Gmaj7/B**
   What if I, what if I?

Bury me, bury me.

Lord Don't Slow Me Down

Words & Music by
Noel Gallagher

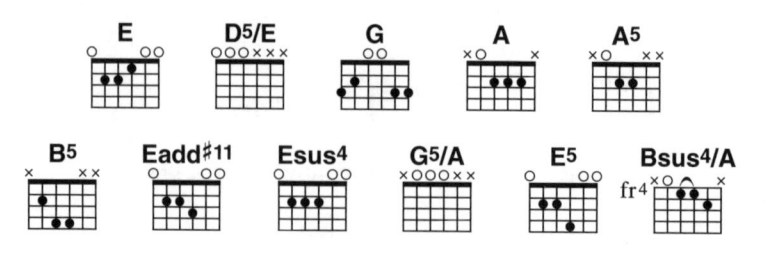

Capo 2nd fret

Intro   ‖: E   D5/E E   G   A   :‖ *play 8 times*

Verse 1
            E   D5/E E   D5/E
            Well, I'm tired   and I'm sick,
            E   D5/E E   D5/E
            Got a habit that I just can't kick.
              E   D5/E   E
            I feel hungover and I'm all in love,
            D5/E   E
            Let the lights go down,
              D5/E   E   D5/E
            I'm gonna shoot 'em up.

Pre-chorus 1
            A5   G   A5   G
            It's alright,   don't be afraid,
                      E   D5/E E
            You gotta keep dreaming in the bed you made,
                B5
            And if it tastes like shit,
                A5
            Well, it beats sleeping rough on the floor.

Link

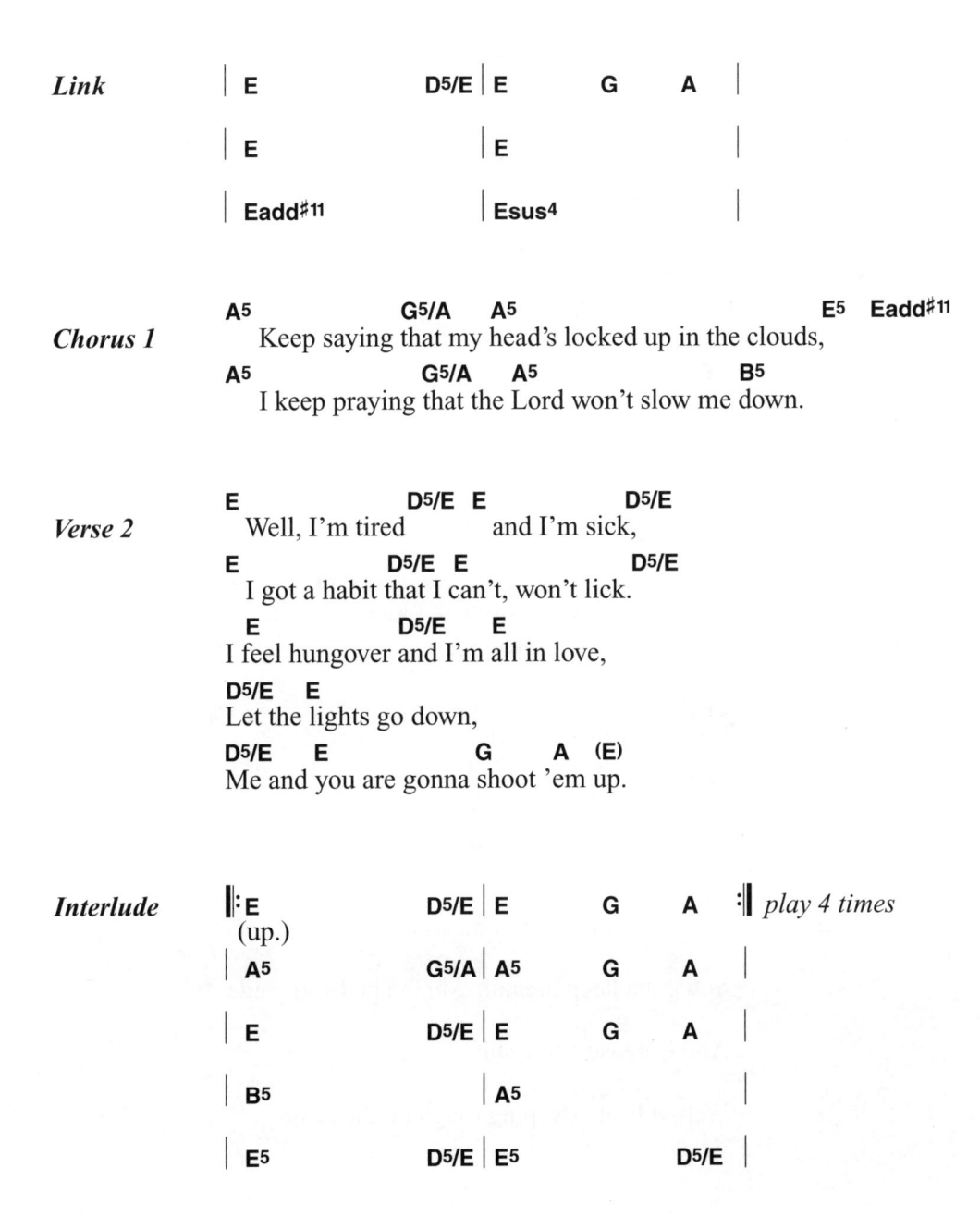

E　　　　　　　　D5/E	E　　　　G　　　A
E	E
Eadd♯11	Esus4

Chorus 1

　　　A5　　　　　　G5/A　　A5　　　　　　　　　　　　E5　　Eadd♯11
　　　　Keep saying that my head's locked up in the clouds,
　　A5　　　　　　G5/A　　A5　　　　　　　　　B5
　　　　I keep praying that the Lord won't slow me down.

Verse 2

　　E　　　　　　D5/E　E　　　　　　D5/E
　　　Well, I'm tired　　　and I'm sick,
　　E　　　　　D5/E　E　　　　　　D5/E
　　　I got a habit that I can't, won't lick.
　　　E　　　　　D5/E　　E
　　I feel hungover and I'm all in love,
　D5/E　　E
　Let the lights go down,
　D5/E　　　E　　　　　G　　　A　　(E)
　Me and you are gonna shoot 'em up.

Interlude

|: E　　　　　　　D5/E | E　　　　G　　　A :|| *play 4 times*
　(up.)
A5　　　　　　G5/A	A5　　　　G　　　A
E　　　　　　　D5/E	E　　　　G　　　A
B5	A5
E5　　　　　　　D5/E	E5　　　　　　　D5/E

Chorus 2

    A5   G5/A   A5   E5   Eadd#11
Keep saying that my head's locked up in the clouds,
  A5   G5/A   A5   B5   Bsus4/A
I keep praying that the Lord won't slow me down.

Verse 3

  E   D5/E E   D5/E
Well, I'm tired   and I'm sick,
  E   D5/E E   D5/E
Got a habit that I just can't kick.
      E   D5/E   E
I feel hungover and I'm all in love,
D5/E   E
When the lights go down,
D5/E   E   G   A   (E)
Me and you are gonna shoot 'em up.

Outro

‖: E   D5/E | E   G   A :‖ *play 4 times*
(up.)

‖: E5 | E5   :‖ *play 4 times*

| E5   :‖

Long Road To Ruin

Words & Music by
Dave Grohl, Taylor Hawkins, Nate Mendel & Chris Shiflett

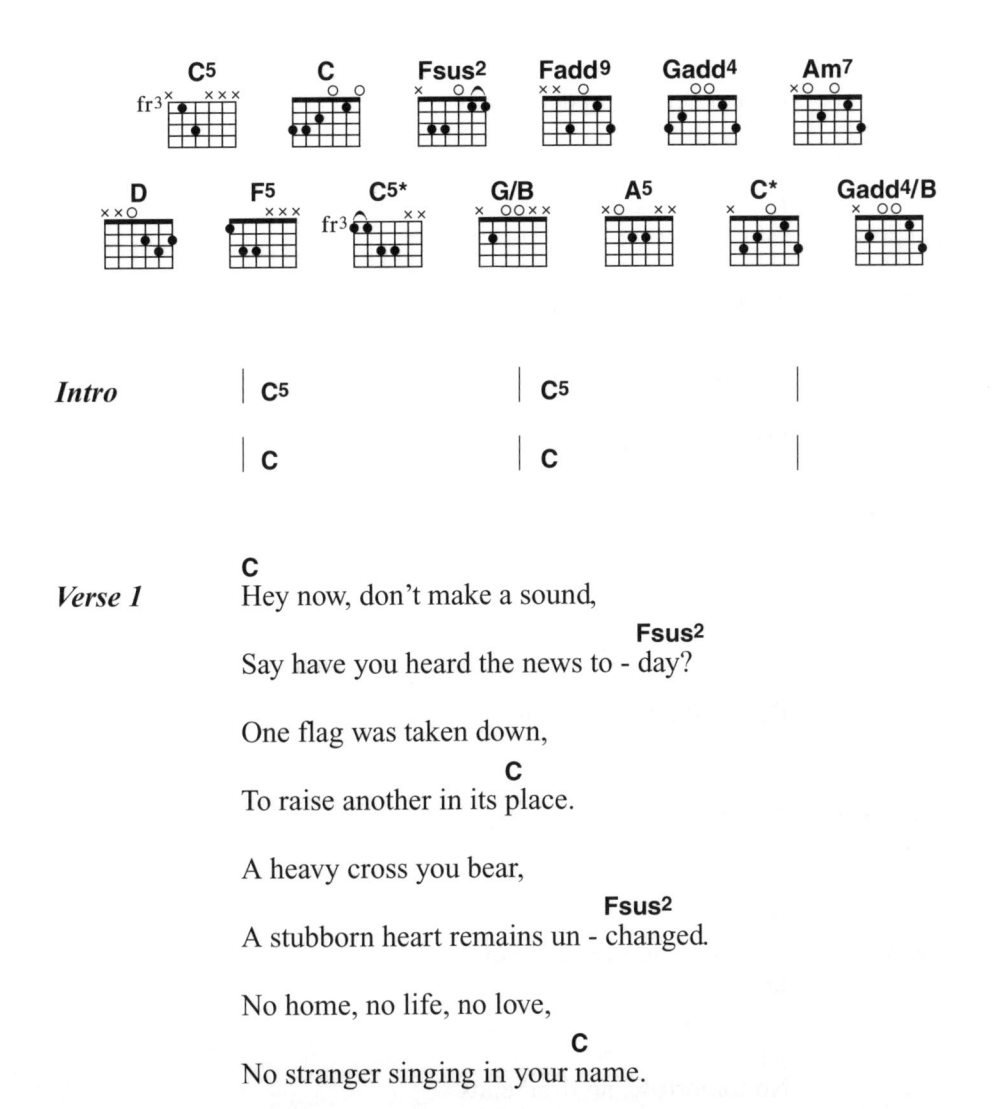

Intro | C5 | C5 |
         | C | C |

Verse 1
    C
Hey now, don't make a sound,
                         Fsus2
Say have you heard the news to - day?

One flag was taken down,
                C
To raise another in its place.

A heavy cross you bear,
                      Fsus2
A stubborn heart remains un - changed.

No home, no life, no love,
                C
No stranger singing in your name.

Pre-Chorus 1
   Fadd9   **Gadd4**
Maybe the season,
     Am7   **Gadd4**
The colours change in the valley skies.
  Fadd9   **Gadd4**
Dear God I've sealed my fate,
  Am7   **D**
Running through hell, heaven can wait.

© Copyright 2007 Universal/MCA Music Limited (87.5%)/Bug Music Limited (12.5%).
All rights in Germany administered by Universal/MCA Music Publ. GmbH.
All Rights Reserved. International Copyright Secured.

Chorus 1

    F5   **C5***
Long road to ruin there in your eyes,
  F5   **C5***   **G/B**
Under the cold street - lights.
A5   **D**   **F5**
No tomorrow, no dead end in sight.

Verse 2

  C
  Let's say we take this town,
                    Fsus2
No king or queen of any state.

Get up to shut it down,
                      C
Open the streets and raise the gates.

I know one wall to scale,
                    Fsus2
I know a field without a name.

Head on without a care,

Before it's way too late.

Pre-Chorus 2 As Pre-Chorus 1

Chorus 2

  F5   **C5***
Long road to ruin there in your eyes,
  F5   **C5***   **G/B**
Under the cold street - lights.
A5   **D**
No tomorrow, no dead ends.
  F5   **C5***
Long road to ruin there in your eyes,
  F5   **C5***   **G/B**
Under the cold street - lights.
A5   **D**   **F5**
No tomorrow, no dead end in sight.

Interlude 1 | **C*** | **Gadd4/B** |

                   | **C*** | **Gadd4/B** |

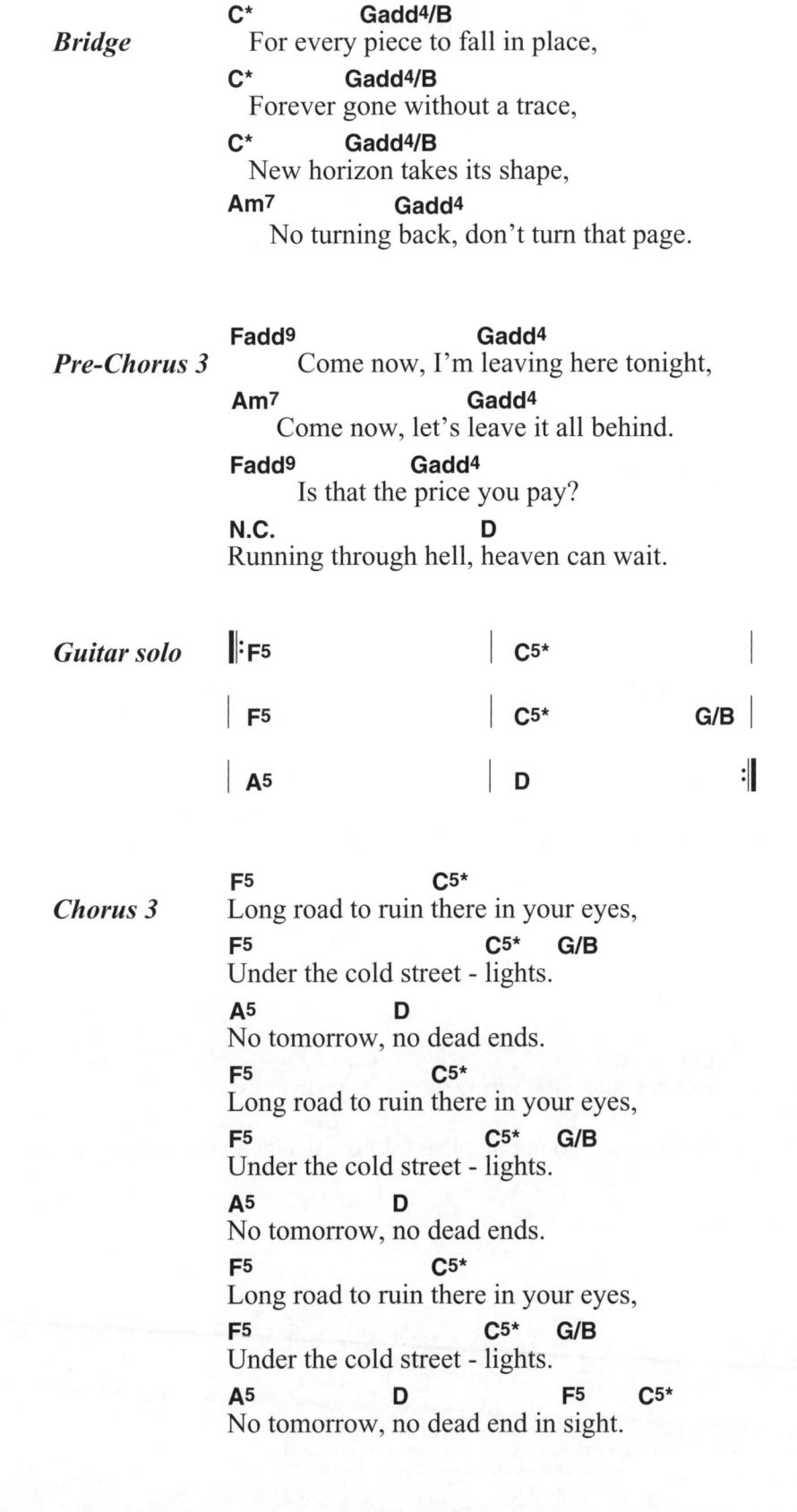

Bridge

C*   Gadd4/B
For every piece to fall in place,
C*   Gadd4/B
Forever gone without a trace,
C*   Gadd4/B
New horizon takes its shape,
Am7   Gadd4
No turning back, don't turn that page.

Pre-Chorus 3

Fadd9   Gadd4
Come now, I'm leaving here tonight,
Am7   Gadd4
Come now, let's leave it all behind.
Fadd9   Gadd4
Is that the price you pay?
N.C.   D
Running through hell, heaven can wait.

Guitar solo

‖: F5 | C5* | |
| F5 | C5* | G/B |
| A5 | D   :‖

Chorus 3

F5   C5*
Long road to ruin there in your eyes,
F5   C5*   G/B
Under the cold street - lights.
A5   D
No tomorrow, no dead ends.
F5   C5*
Long road to ruin there in your eyes,
F5   C5*   G/B
Under the cold street - lights.
A5   D
No tomorrow, no dead ends.
F5   C5*
Long road to ruin there in your eyes,
F5   C5*   G/B
Under the cold street - lights.
A5   D   F5   C5*
No tomorrow, no dead end in sight.

Love's Not A Competition
(But I'm Winning)

Words & Music by
Nicholas Hodgson, Richard Wilson, Andrew White,
James Rix & Nicholas Baines

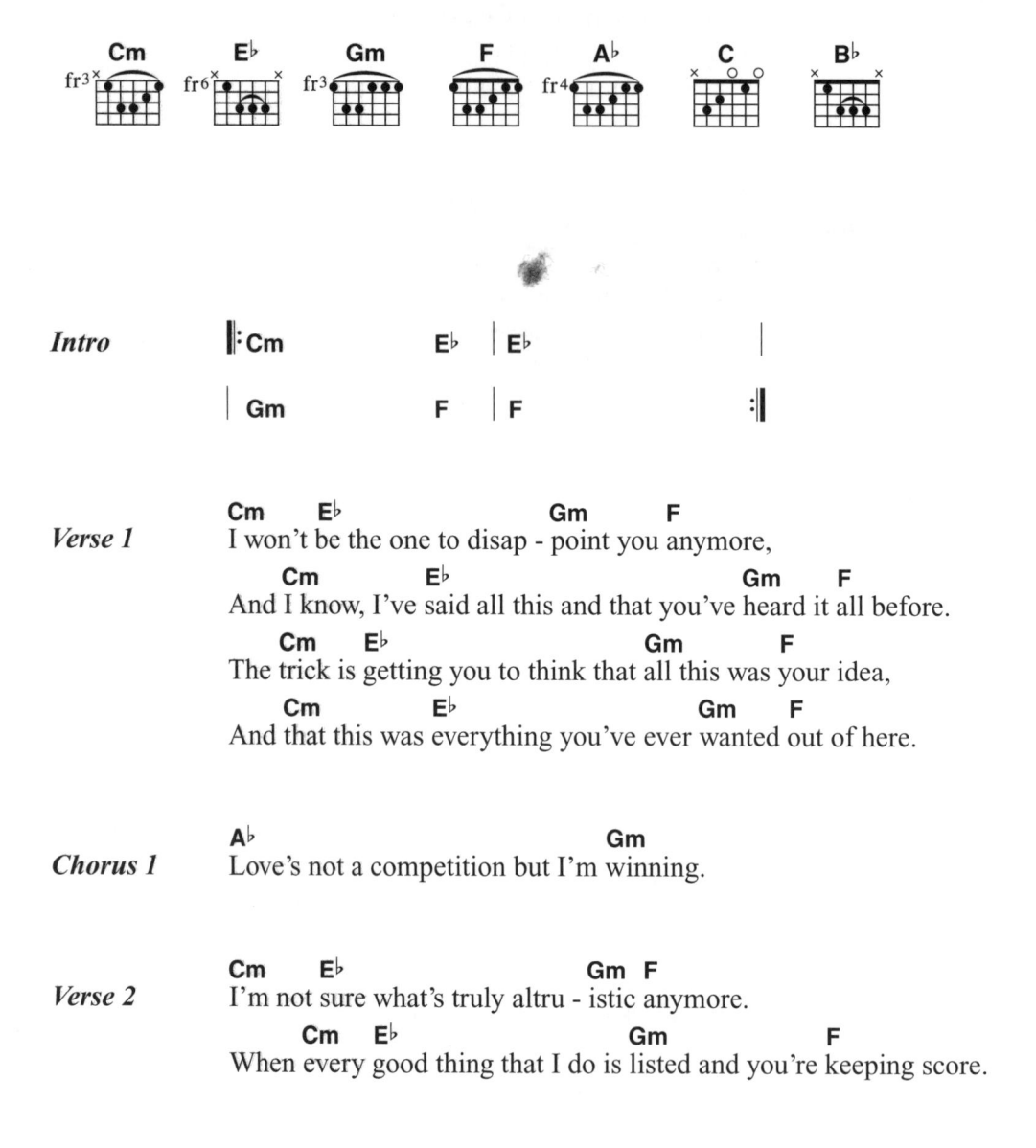

Cm   E♭   Gm   F   A♭   C   B♭

Intro   ‖: Cm   E♭ | E♭ |
            | Gm   F | F   :‖

Verse 1
     Cm   E♭   Gm   F
I won't be the one to disap - point you anymore,
     Cm   E♭   Gm   F
And I know, I've said all this and that you've heard it all before.
     Cm   E♭   Gm   F
The trick is getting you to think that all this was your idea,
     Cm   E♭   Gm   F
And that this was everything you've ever wanted out of here.

Chorus 1
     A♭   Gm
Love's not a competition but I'm winning.

Verse 2
     Cm   E♭   Gm F
I'm not sure what's truly altru - istic anymore.
     Cm   E♭   Gm   F
When every good thing that I do is listed and you're keeping score.

© Copyright 2006 Rondor Music (London) Limited.
All rights in Germany administered by Rondor Musikverlag GmbH.
All Rights Reserved. International Copyright Secured.

Chorus 2

  A♭   **Gm**
Love's not a competition but I'm winning,
 A♭   **Gm**
Love's not a competition but I'm winning.

Bridge

       C   **B♭**
At least I thought I was but there's no way of knowing,
       C   **B♭**
At least I thought I was but there's no way of knowing.
    A♭   **Gm**   **F**
You know what it's like when you're new to the game but I'm not.

Interlude

‖: Cm   E♭ | E♭ |
| Gm   F | F   :‖

Outro

 Cm **E♭**   **Gm**   **F**
‖: I won't be the one to disap - point you,
Cm **E♭**   **Gm**   **F**
I won't be the one to disap - point you anymore. :‖ *repeat to fade*

Make It Wit Chu

Words & Music by
Josh Homme, Alain Johannes & Mickey Melchiando

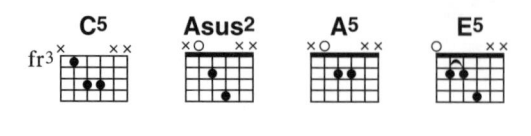

| C5 | Asus2 | A5 | E5 |

Intro   ‖: C5 | Asus2 A5 |
        | E5 | E5   :‖ *play 4 times*

Verse 1
      C5   Asus2
You wanna know if I know why?
A5   E5
I can't say that I do.
      C5   Asus2
Don't understand the evil eye,
A5   E5
Or how one becomes two.
      C5   Asus2
I just can't recall what started it all,
A5   E5
Or how to begin in the end.
      C5
I ain't here to break it,
      Asus2   A5   E5
Just see how far it will bend,

Again and again, again and again.

Chorus 1
      C5
    I wanna make it,
Asus2   A5   E5
    I wan - na make it wit chu,

Anytime, anywhere.
      C5
    I wanna make it,
Asus2   A5   E5
    I wan - na make it wit chu.

© Copyright 2003 Copyright Control/Board Stiff Music/Channel This Music/Famous Music LLC.
Universal Music Publishing Limited (75%)/Famous Music Publishing Limited (12.5%)/Copyright Control (12.5%).
All rights in Germany administered by Universal Music Publ. GmbH.
All Rights Reserved. International Copyright Secured.

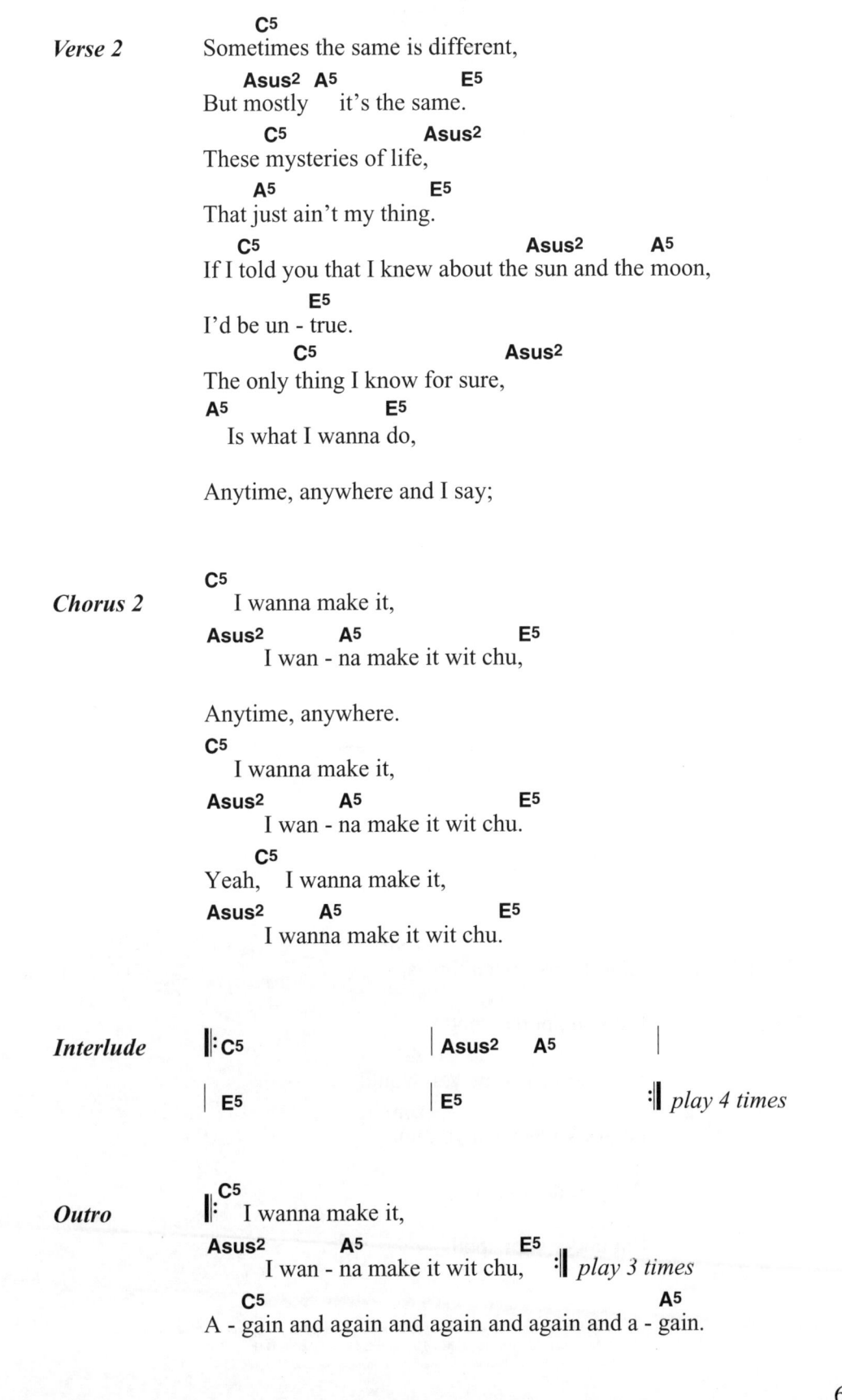

Verse 2

       C5
Sometimes the same is different,
     Asus2 A5   **E5**
But mostly   it's the same.
       C5   **Asus2**
These mysteries of life,
   A5   **E5**
That just ain't my thing.
      C5   **Asus2**   **A5**
If I told you that I knew about the sun and the moon,
       E5
I'd be un - true.
      C5   **Asus2**
The only thing I know for sure,
A5   **E5**
  Is what I wanna do,

Anytime, anywhere and I say;

Chorus 2

    C5
   I wanna make it,
Asus2   **A5**   **E5**
  I wan - na make it wit chu,

Anytime, anywhere.
C5
   I wanna make it,
Asus2   **A5**   **E5**
  I wan - na make it wit chu.
   C5
Yeah, I wanna make it,
Asus2   **A5**   **E5**
  I wanna make it wit chu.

Interlude

‖: **C5** | **Asus2** **A5** |

| **E5** | **E5**   :‖ *play 4 times*

Outro

    C5
‖: I wanna make it,
Asus2   **A5**   **E5**
  I wan - na make it wit chu, :‖ *play 3 times*
   C5   **A5**
A - gain and again and again and again and a - gain.

Mercy

Words & Music by
Stephen Booker & Aimee Duffy

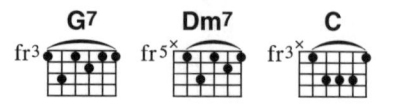

G7 Dm7 C

Intro ‖: (G) | (G)   :‖

(G) (C/G) (G7) (C/G)
‖: Yeah, yeah, yeah,

(G) (C/G) (G7) (C/G)
Yeah, yeah, yeah. :‖

| Dm7 | C |
| G7 | G7 |

Verse 1

G7
I love you,

But I gotta stay true.

My moral's got me on my knees,

I'm begging please,

Stop playing games.

Pre-Chorus 1
          Dm7
I don't know what this is,
   C
But you got me good,
          G7
Just like you knew you would.
         Dm7
I don't know what you do,
   C
But you do it well,
      G7
I'm under your spell.

© Copyright 2008 EMI Music Publishing Limited (60%)/Universal Music Publishing Limited (40%).
All rights in Germany administered by Universal Music Publ. GmbH.
All Rights Reserved. International Copyright Secured.

Chorus 1

                                G7
You got me begging you for mercy,

Why won't you release me?
                              C
You got me begging you for mercy,
                G7
Why won't you re - lease me?
         Dm7 **C** **G7**
I said re - lease__ me.

Verse 2

  G7
    Now you think that I,

Will be something on the side.

But you got to understand,

That I need a man,

Who can take my hand, yes I do.

Pre-Chorus 2   As Pre-Chorus 1

Chorus 2

                                G7
You got me begging you for mercy,

Why won't you release me?
                              C
You got me begging you for mercy,
                G7
Why won't you re - lease me?
                  Dm7   **C**   **G7**
I said you'd better re - lease me__ yeah.__

Bridge

N.C.
I'm begging you for mercy,

Just why won't you release me?

I'm begging you for mercy,

You got me begging,

You got me begging,

You got me begging.

Chorus 3

G7
Mercy, why won't you release me?
C
I'm begging you for mercy,
G7
Why won't you re - lease me?
                         Dm7 C G7
You've got me begging you for mer - cy, yeah.

I'm begging you for mercy,

I'm begging you for mercy,
C
I'm begging you for mercy,
G7
I'm begging you for mercy.
                  Dm7 C G7
Why won't you re - lease___ me, yeah?

Outro

G7
‖: You've got me begging you for mercy,

You got me begging,

Down on my knees. :‖ *repeat ad lib. to fade*

Mouthwash

Words & Music by
Kate Nash

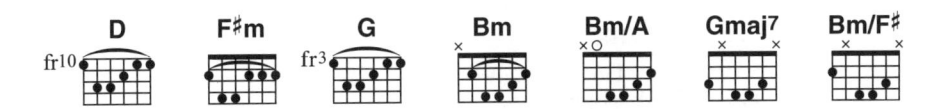

[Chord diagrams: D (fr10), F♯m, G (fr3), Bm, Bm/A, Gmaj7, Bm/F♯]

To match recording tune all strings down a semitone

Intro

||: D | D |
| F♯m | G   :||

Verse 1

    D   F♯m G
This is my face,
D
Covered in freckles,
                F♯m   G
With the oc - casional spot and some veins.
    D   F♯m G
This is my bod - y,
D
Covered in skin,
               F♯m   G
And not all of it you can see.
        D   F♯m G
And   this is my mind,
           D
It goes over and over,
  F♯m   G
The same old lines.
        D   F♯m G
And   this is my brain,
          D
Its tortuous analytical thoughts,
         F♯m   G
Make me go in - sane.

© Copyright 2007 Universal Music Publishing Limited.
All rights in Germany administered by Universal Music Publ. GmbH.
All Rights Reserved. International Copyright Secured.

Chorus 1

    Bm Bm/A Gmaj7
I   use   mouthwash,

Bm   Bm7/A Gmaj7
Some - times   I   floss,

Bm   Bm7/A Gmaj7
I've got a fami - ly,

               Bm   Bm/A Gmaj7
And I drink cups of tea.

Bm   Bm/A Gmaj7
I've got nos - talgic pavements,

Bm   Bm/A Gmaj7
I've got fa - miliar faces,

Bm   Bm/A   Gmaj7
I've got mixed up memories,

              Bm   Bm/A Gmaj7
And I've got favourite pla - ces.

        Bm   Bm/A   Gmaj7 Bm/F♯
‖: And I'm singing "oh-oh" on a Friday night. :‖

        Bm   Bm/A
‖: And I'm singing "oh-oh" on a Friday night,

    Gmaj7   Bm/F♯
And I hope everything's gonna be alright. :‖

Verse 2

   D   F♯m G
This is my face,

   D
I've got a thousand opinions,

        F♯m   G
And I've got time, I'm trying to ex - plain.

      D   F♯m G
And this is my bod - y,

    D
No matter how you try and disable it,

  F♯m   G
Yes, I'll   still be here.

    D   F♯m   G
And this is my   mind,—

   D
And   although you try to infringe,

F♯m   G
You cannot confine.

    D   F♯m G
And this is my brain,—

   D
And even if you try and hold me back,

        F♯m   G
There's noth - ing that you can gain.

Chorus 2

     Bm Bm/A Gmaj7
    Because I use mouthwash,
Bm **Bm7/A Gmaj7**
Some - times I floss,
Bm   **Bm7/A Gmaj7**
I've got a fami - ly,
     Bm **Bm/A Gmaj7**
And I drink cups of tea.
Bm   **Bm/A Gmaj7**
I've got nos - talgic pavements,
Bm   **Bm/A Gmaj7**
I've got fa - miliar faces,
Bm **Bm/A** **Gmaj7**
I've got mixed up memories,
      Bm **Bm/A Gmaj7**
And I've got favourite pla - ces.
   Bm   **Bm/A**   **Gmaj7 Bm/F#**
‖: And I'm singing "oh-oh" on a Friday night. :‖
   Bm   **Bm/A**
‖: And I'm singing "oh-oh" on a Friday night,
 Gmaj7   **Bm/F#**
And I hope everything's gonna be alright. :‖
 Bm **Bm/A**
‖: Oh, oh, oh, oh, oh, oh,
Gmaj7 **Bm/F#**
Oh, oh, oh, oh, oh, oh, oh. :‖ *play 8 times*

Outro   ‖: **Bm** | **Bm/A** |

      | **Gmaj7** | **Bm/F#**   :‖ *play 4 times*

      | **Bm**   ‖

Moving To New York

Words & Music by
Matthew Murphy, Daniel Haggis & Tord Knudson

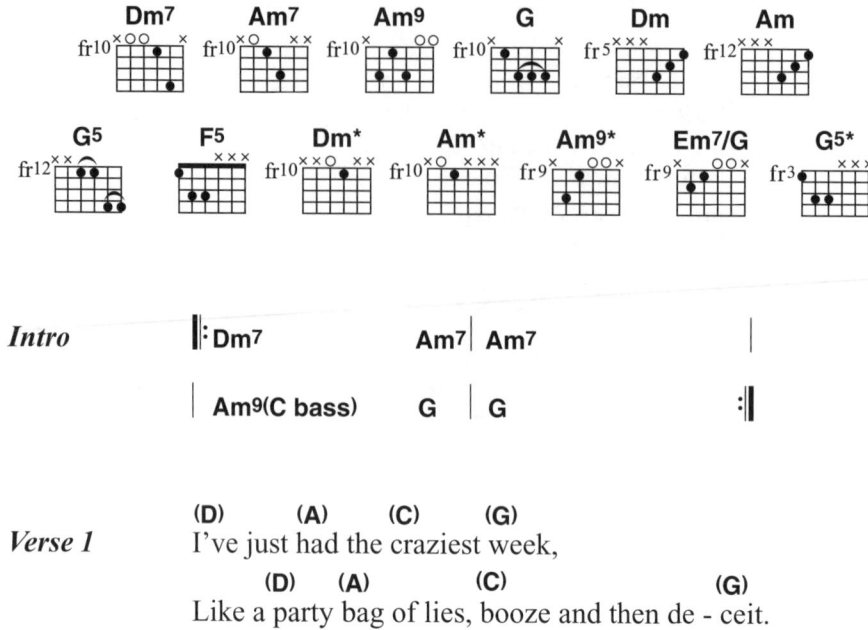

[Chord diagrams: Dm7, Am7, Am9, G, Dm, Am, G5, F5, Dm*, Am*, Am9*, Em7/G, G5*]

Intro

‖: Dm7   Am7 | Am7 |
| Am9(C bass) G | G   :‖

Verse 1

    (D)   (A)   (C)   (G)
I've just had the craziest week,
              (D)   (A)   (C)   (G)
Like a party bag of lies, booze and then de - ceit.
        Dm   Am   Am(C bass) G5
And I don't know why I want to voice this out loud,
Dm   Am   Am(C bass) G5
   It's theraputic somehow.

Chorus 1

       Dm7   Am7(C bass)
So I'm moving to New York,
       Am9   G
'Cause I've got problems with my sleep.
      Dm7   Am7
And we're not the same,
  Am9(C bass)   G
And I will wear that on my sleeve.
       Dm7(F bass)   Am7(C bass)
So I'm moving to New York,
       Am9   G
'Cause I've got issues with my sleep.
      Dm7   Am7
Looks like Christmas came early,
Am9(C bass)   G
Christmas came early for me.

© 2006 Universal Music Publishing Limited.
All rights in Germany administered by Universal Music Publ. GmbH.
All Rights Reserved. International Copyright Secured.

Link   ‖: F5 | F5   :‖

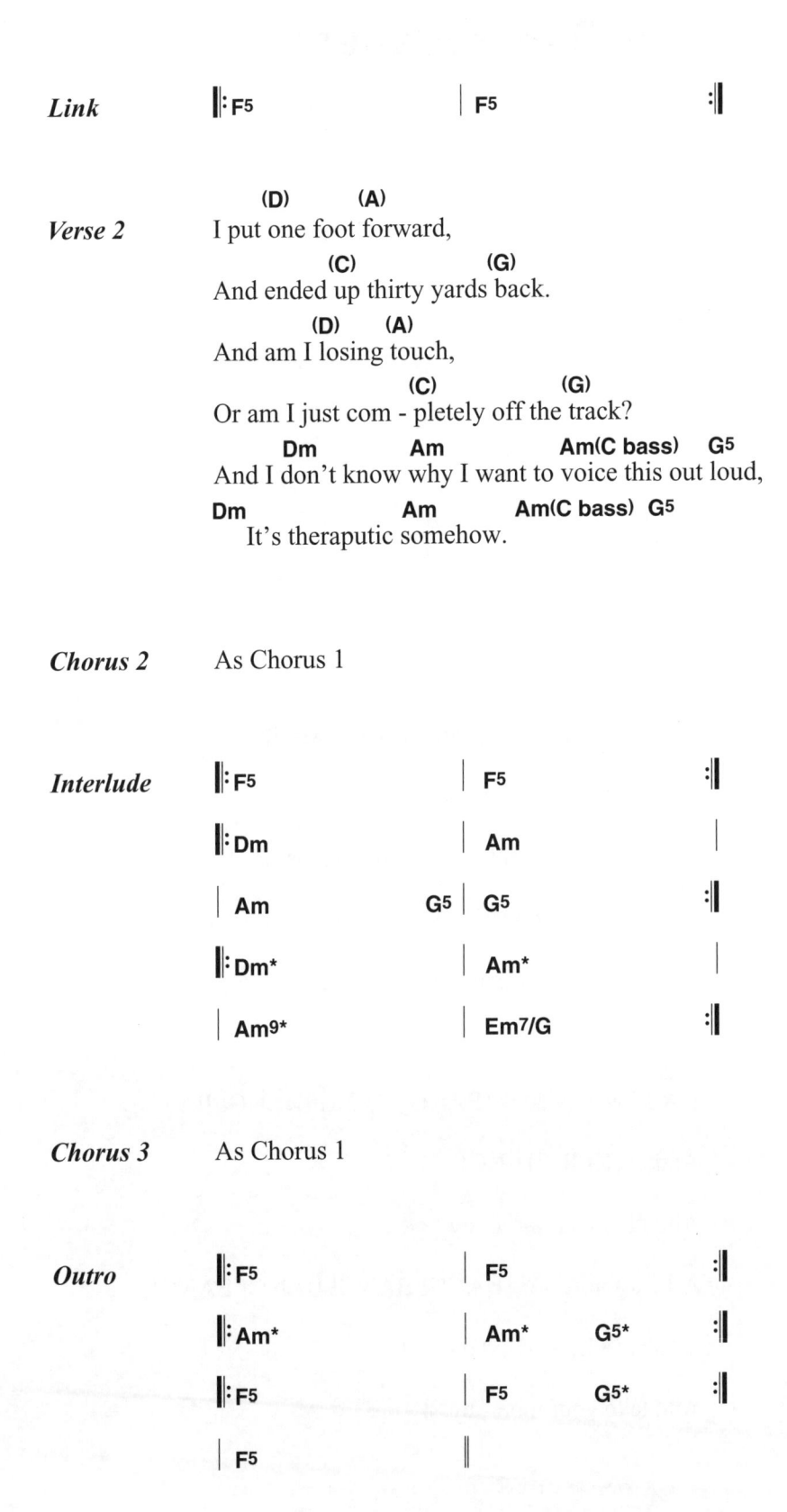

Verse 2
        (D)   **(A)**
I put one foot forward,
          (C)   **(G)**
And ended up thirty yards back.
      (D)   **(A)**
And am I losing touch,
              (C)   **(G)**
Or am I just com - pletely off the track?
    Dm   **Am**   **Am(C bass)** **G5**
And I don't know why I want to voice this out loud,
Dm   **Am**   **Am(C bass)** **G5**
   It's theraputic somehow.

Chorus 2   As Chorus 1

Interlude   ‖: F5 | F5   :‖

             ‖: Dm | Am |

             | Am   G5 | G5   :‖

             ‖: Dm* | Am* |

             | Am9* | Em7/G   :‖

Chorus 3   As Chorus 1

Outro   ‖: F5 | F5   :‖

            ‖: Am* | Am*   G5*   :‖

            ‖: F5 | F5   G5*   :‖

            | F5   ‖

Paper Planes

Words & Music by
Mick Jones, Joe Strummer, Paul Simonon, Topper Headon,
Thomas Pentz & Mathangi Arulpragasam

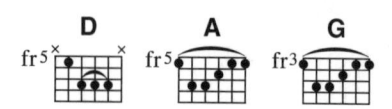

D A G

Intro | D | D   A |
       | G | G |

Verse 1

‖: D
I fly like paper, get high like planes,

                A
If you catch me at the border I got visas in my name.

    G
If you come around here, I make 'em all day,

I get one down in a second if you wait. :‖

‖: D
Sometimes I feel sitting on trains,

            A
Every stop I get to I'm clocking that game.

G
Everyone's a winner now we're making our fame,

Bona fide hustler making my name. :‖

Chorus 1

‖: D
All I wanna do is (BANG! BANG! BANG! BANG!)

And… (KER-CHING!)

       A
And take your mon - ey.

G
All I wanna do is (BANG! BANG! BANG! BANG!)

And… (KER-CHING!)

       A
And take your mon - ey. :‖

© Copyright 2007 Universal Music Publishing Limited (50%)/
Zomba Music Publishers Limited (25%)/Domino Publishing Company (25%).
All rights in Germany administered by Universal Music Publ. GmbH.
All Rights Reserved. International Copyright Secured.

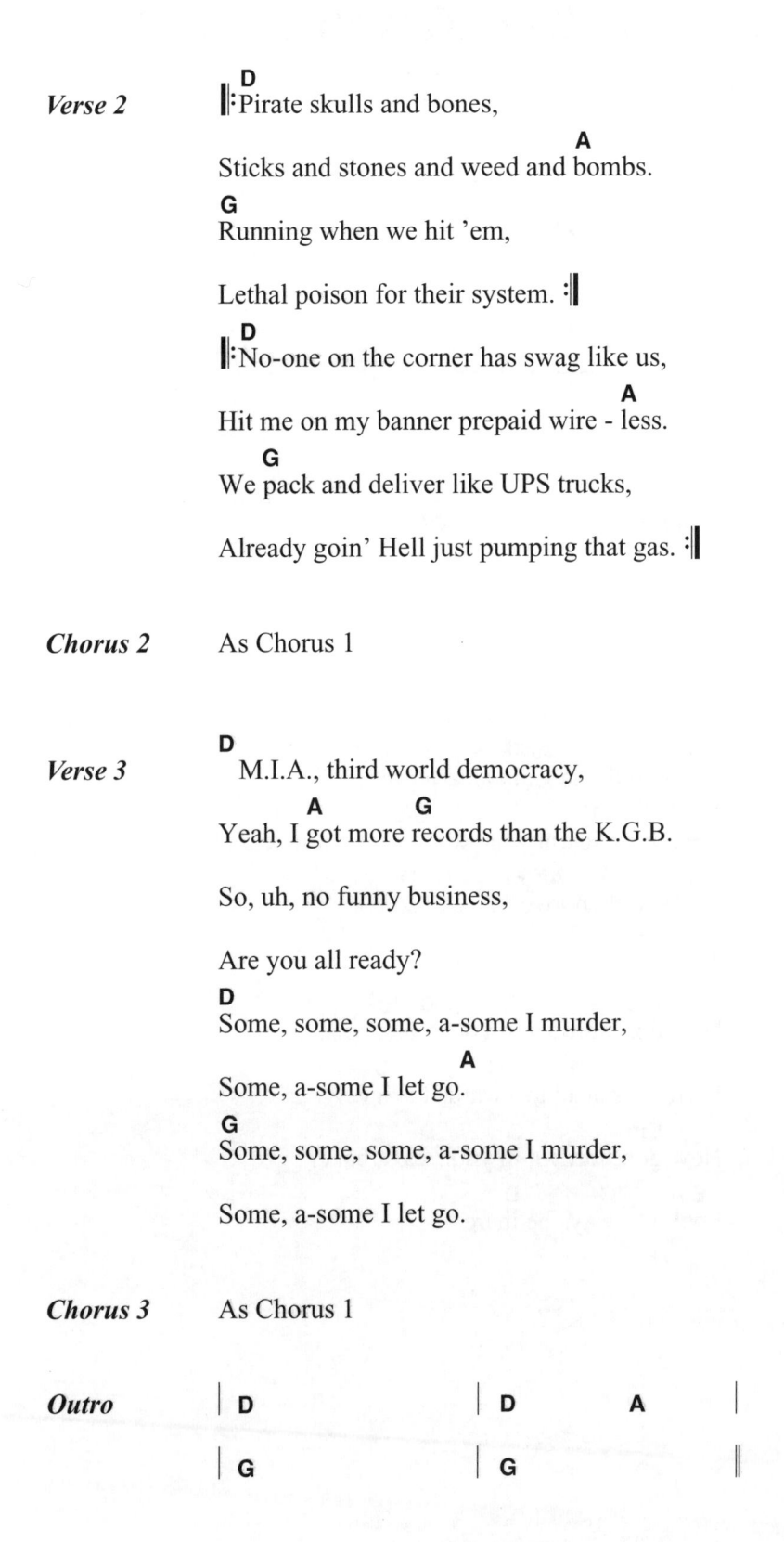

Verse 2

‖: **D**
Pirate skulls and bones,

                              A
Sticks and stones and weed and bombs.
G
Running when we hit 'em,

Lethal poison for their system. :‖

‖: **D**
No-one on the corner has swag like us,

                              A
Hit me on my banner prepaid wire - less.
  G
We pack and deliver like UPS trucks,

Already goin' Hell just pumping that gas. :‖

Chorus 2   As Chorus 1

Verse 3

D
   M.I.A., third world democracy,
     A   **G**
Yeah, I got more records than the K.G.B.

So, uh, no funny business,

Are you all ready?
D
Some, some, some, a-some I murder,
             A
Some, a-some I let go.
G
Some, some, some, a-some I murder,

Some, a-some I let go.

Chorus 3   As Chorus 1

Outro | D | D   A |

               | G | G   ‖

Push Your Head Towards The Air

Words & Music by
Tom Smith, Russell Leetch, Chris Urbanowicz & Ed Lay

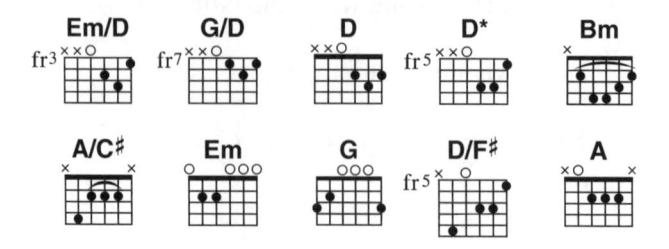

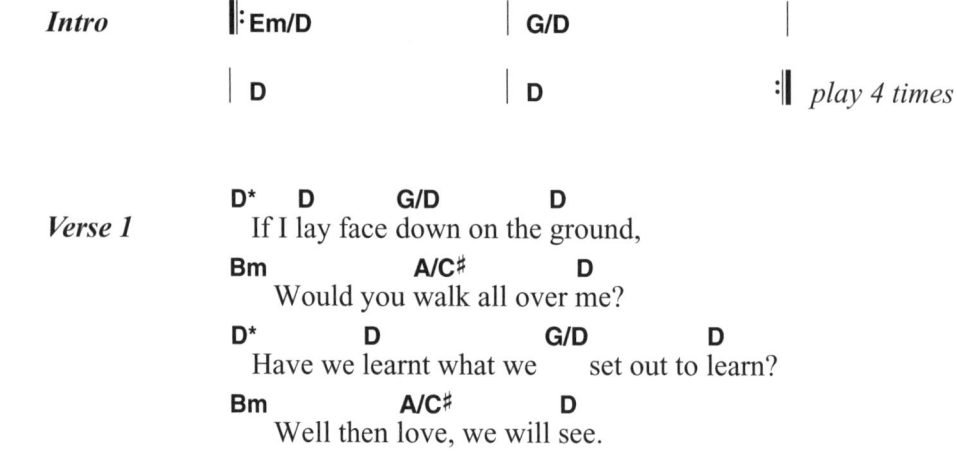

Intro   ‖: Em/D | G/D |
            | D | D   :‖ *play 4 times*

Verse 1
    D*   D   G/D   D
If I lay face down on the ground,
  Bm   A/C#   D
Would you walk all over me?
  D*   D   G/D   D
Have we learnt what we   set out to learn?
  Bm   A/C#   D
Well then love, we will see.

Chorus 1
     Em   G   D
Now don't drown in your tears, babe,
        Em   G   D
Push your head to - wards the air.
     Em   G   D
Now don't drown in your tears, babe,
  Em   G   D
I will al - ways be there.

© Copyright 2007 Soul Kitchen Music Limited.
Kobalt Music Publishing Limited.
All Rights Reserved. International Copyright Secured.

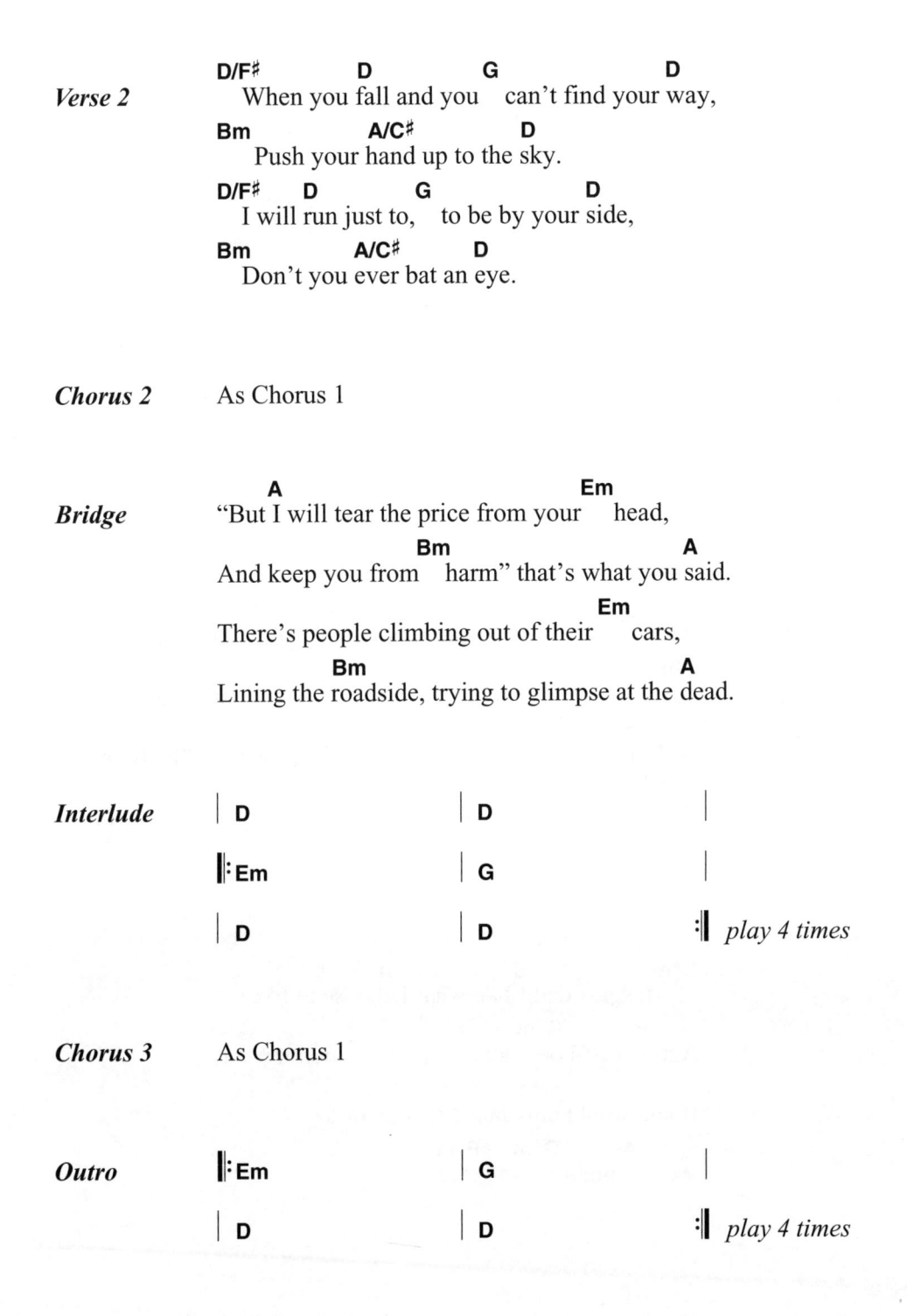

Verse 2

```
         D/F#        D          G              D
     When you fall and you   can't find your way,
     Bm           A/C#         D
        Push your hand up to the sky.
     D/F#   D        G              D
        I will run just to,  to be by your side,
     Bm            A/C#        D
        Don't you ever bat an eye.
```

Chorus 2   As Chorus 1

Bridge

```
            A                          Em
     "But I will tear the price from your   head,
                     Bm                    A
      And keep you from   harm" that's what you said.
                                         Em
      There's people climbing out of their   cars,
                   Bm                       A
      Lining the roadside, trying to glimpse at the dead.
```

Interlude

D	D	
:Em	G	
D	D	:| play 4 times

Chorus 3   As Chorus 1

Outro

|:Em | G | |
| D | D | :\| play 4 times |

Romantic Type

Words & Music by
Oliver Main & Matthew Bowman

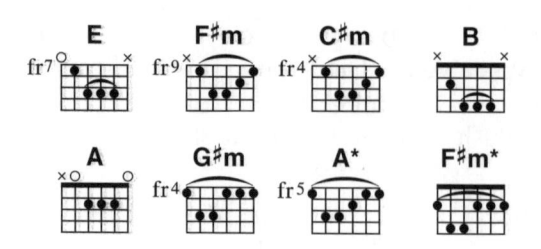

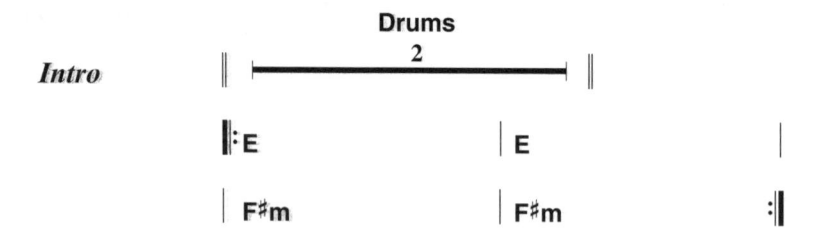

[Chord diagrams: E (fr7), F#m (fr9), C#m (fr4), B, A, G#m (fr4), A* (fr5), F#m*]

Intro

|| Drums 2 ||

|: E | E |
| F#m | F#m   :|

Verse 1
     E
Well, I can see you standing there like you know what to do,
F#m
You all think you know me but you haven't got a clue.
     E
Well, I can see you looking but you're looking at the floor,
   F#m
But I don't think I really care because you paid at the door.

Chorus 1
  C#m   B   A   B
And it's not that I'm not the ro - mantic type,
C#m   B   A
It's just that I like what I choose to like.
 B   G#m   A*
And if you'd only take the time to look my way,
     G#m
If you would only take the time to see,
   A*   G#m   F#m*
Well, I might let you stay.

© Copyright 2007 Universal Music Publishing MGB Limited.
All Rights in Germany Administered by Musik Edition Discoton GmbH
(A Division of Universal Music Publishing Group).
All Rights Reserved. International Copyright Secured.

Interlude | E | E |
             | F♯m | F♯m |

Verse 2
E
I know that you want something and you want it from me,
F♯m
Everyone says we're the same but I just cannot see.
        E
And I know what you're asking for 'cause I've just read the sign,
        F♯m
Would paying once or maybe twice be really such a crime?

Chorus 2
        C♯m   B   A   B
            And it's not that I'm not the ro - mantic type,
        C♯m   B   A
            It's just that I like what I choose to like.
          B   G♯m   A*
And if you'd only take the time to look my way,
              G♯m
If you would only take the time to see,
            A*   G♯m   F♯m*   B
Well, I might let you stay.

Interlude ‖: E | E |
             | F♯m | F♯m   :‖ *play 4 times*

Outro
        C♯m   B   A   B
            It's not that I'm not the ro - mantic type,
        C♯m   B   A
            It's just that I like what I choose to like.
        C♯m   B   A   B
            It's not that I'm not the ro - mantic type,
        C♯m   B   A   B   E
            It's just that I like what I choose to like.

Run

Words by Thomas Callaway & Brian Burton
Music by Keith Mansfield, Thomas Callaway & Brian Burton

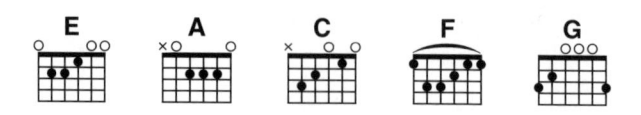

E   A   C   F   G

Intro | E   A   C   F | E |
          | E | |

Verse 1

    E   G
Yeah, it's still the same,   can't you feel the pain?
  A   G
When the needle hits the vein,   ain't nothing like the real thing.
  E
I've seen it once before,

And oh, it's something else, good God.

                          G
Cool breeze, come on in,   sunshine come on down,
  A
These are the tear drops of the clown,
  G
Circus coming to town.
  E
All I'm saying is sometimes I'm more scared of myself.

You better move, I said move.

Chorus 1

    E   G
Runaway, runaway,
A   G   E
Run children,   run for your life.
                G
Runaway, runaway,
A   G
Run children, oh!
E   N.C.   E
Here it comes, said run, al - right!

Verse 2

   E
Yeah I'm on the run,
G
See where I'm coming from.
A
When you see me coming run,
G
Before you see what I'm running from.
E
No time for question asking time is passing by, alright!
                   G
You can't win child,   we've all tried to,
A   G
You've been lied to,   it's all ready inside you.
E
Either you run right now,

Or you best get ready to die.

You better move, I said move.

Chorus 2

    E   G
Runaway, runaway,
A   G   E
Run children,   run for your life.
                G
Runaway, runaway,
A   G
Run children, oh!
E   N.C.
Here it comes, said run.

Bridge

  E
Hurry little children,
  C
Run this way,
  E **F** **E**
I have got a beast at bay.___
       G
Oh, promise me, when the chance comes,
 A   **G**
 You'll run as fast as you can.
 E   **G**
Don't you dare look backwards,
 A   **G** **E**
 Run as fast as you can.___

Link | E | E |

Interlude
  E **G**
‖: La, la-la, la-la, la,
 A **G**
 La, la-la, la,
  E
La, la-la, la, la-la. :‖
E
 Ooh-ooh.

Chorus 3
  E   **G**
 Runaway, runaway,
 A   **G**   **E**
 Run children, run for your life.
     G
Runaway, runaway,
 A   **G**
 Run children, oh!
E   **N.C.**
Here it comes, said run.

The Step And The Walk

**Words & Music by
Liela Moss, Toby Butler, Luke Ford, Daniel Higgins & Oliver Betts**

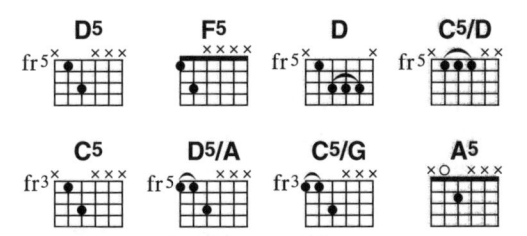

Intro

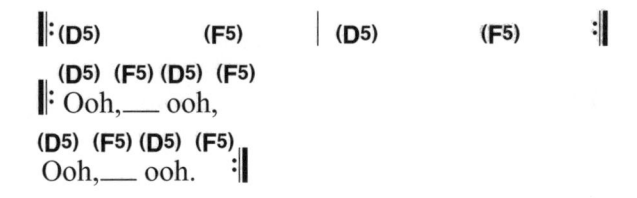

‖: (D5)　　　(F5)　　│(D5)　　　(F5)　　:‖

(D5) (F5) (D5) (F5)
‖: Ooh,— ooh,
(D5) (F5) (D5) (F5)
Ooh,— ooh. :‖

Verse 1

(D5)　　　(F5) (D5)　　　(F5) (D5)　　　(F5) (D5)
Ten Eng - lish pounds and this hard pave - ment feels,
　(F5)　　　(D5)
As though I'm moving to the end,
(F5)　　(D5)　　　　　(F5)　　(D5) (F5) (D5) (F5)
Am I moving to the end of your lov - ing?_____
D　　　C5/D　D　　C5/D
How, how did I do this?
D　　　　　　C5/D　　D　　C5/D
Me, I put the wall a - round my heart.
D　C5/D　　D　C5/D　D　　　　C5/D　　　D
Why didn't I no - tice such a cold detach - ment from the start?
C5/D　　D
Oh, the joys they slammed down,
C5/D　　D　　　　　C5/D　D　　　　　C5/D　D
And no-one in this town burns bright enough.

© Copyright 2007 Universal Music Publishing MGB Limited.
All Rights in Germany Administered by Musik Edition Discoton GmbH
(A Division of Universal Music Publishing Group).
All Rights Reserved. International Copyright Secured.

Chorus 1

          D5   **C5** **D5**
Without joy, joy, joy in the rain,
C5   **D5/A**   **C5/G D5/A**
I could feel forever the   same.
    C5 D5   **C5**   **D5**
With - out joy, joy, joy in the rain,
C5   **D5/A**   **C5/G D5/A**
I could feel forever the   same.

Link 1   ‖: **D5**   **F5** | **D5**   **F5**   :‖

Verse 2

      D   **C5/D D**
So how, how did I do this?
C5/D **D**   **C5/D**   **D**
Oh   me, I put that box a - round my heart.
C5/D   **D**   **C5/D**   **D C5/D D**   **C5/D**   **D**
    Why   could - n't I no - tice such a cool, detached from the start?
C5/D   **D**
Oh, the joys they slammed down,
C5/D   **D**   **C5/D** **D**   **C5/D** **D**
For no-one in this town is right   enough.___

Chorus 2

          D5   **C5** **D5**
Without joy, joy, joy in the rain,
C5   **D5/A**   **C5/G D5/A**
I could feel forever the   same.
    C5 D5   **C5**   **D5**
With - out joy, joy, joy in the rain,
C5   **D5/A**   **C5/G D5/A**
I could feel forever the   same.

Interlude ‖: D5   C5   A5 | A5   C5   A5 |
| D5   C5   A5 | A5   C5   :‖
‖: D5   (C bass) | (B bass)   (A bass) :‖
| D5   C5   D5 | D5   C5   D5/A |
| D5/A   C5/G   D5/A | D5/A   C5   D5 |
           (With - out   joy)

Chorus 3
      (C5) (D5)   C5   D5
‖: With - out joy, joy, joy in the rain,
  C5   D5/A   C5/G D5/A
I could feel forever the same.
     C5 D5   C5   D5
With - out joy, joy, joy in the rain,
  C5   D5/A   C5/G D5/A
I could feel forever the same. :‖
C5   D5
Ooh.

Strange Times

Words & Music by
Daniel Auerbach & Patrick Carney

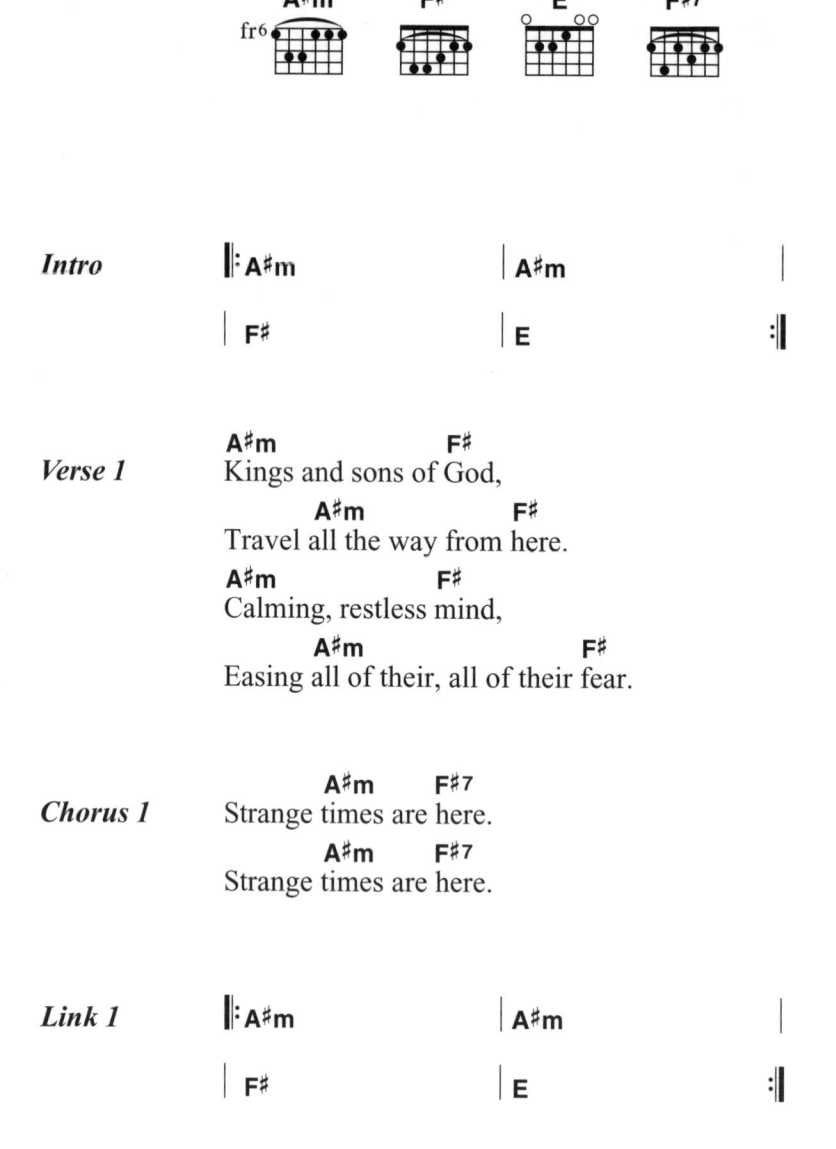

A#m F# E F#7

Intro ‖: A#m | A#m |
          | F# | E   :‖

Verse 1
     A#m   F#
Kings and sons of God,
     A#m   F#
Travel all the way from here.
A#m   F#
Calming, restless mind,
     A#m   F#
Easing all of their, all of their fear.

Chorus 1
     A#m   F#7
Strange times are here.
     A#m   F#7
Strange times are here.

Link 1 ‖: A#m | A#m |
           | F# | E   :‖

© Copyright 2008 Chrysalis Music Limited.
All Rights Reserved. International Copyright Secured.

Verse 2

A♯m   **F♯**
Statue in the square,
A♯m   **F♯**
Meant so much when we first met.
A♯m   **F♯**
People come from far and near,
A♯m   **F♯**
Bless them if, bless them if it would.

Chorus 2   As Chorus 1

Link 2   ‖: **A♯m** | **A♯m** |

             | **F♯** | **E**   :‖

Verse 3

A♯m   **F♯**
Sadie, dry your tear,
A♯m   **F♯**
I will be the one,
A♯m   **F♯**
To pull you through the mirror,
A♯m   **F♯**
Be - fore you come, before you come un - done.

Chorus 3

             A♯m   **F♯7**
‖: Strange times are here.
            A♯m   **F♯7**
Strange times are here. :‖

Outro   ‖: **A♯m** | **A♯m** |

            | **F♯** | **E**   :‖   *play 4 times*

            | **A♯m**   ‖

Teardrop

Words & Music by
Robert Del Naja, Grant Marshall, Andrew Vowles & Elizabeth Fraser

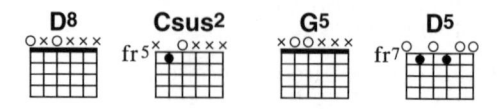

D8   Csus2   G5   D5

Tuning: D♭, G♭, D♭, G♭, A♭, D♭

Verse 1
D8
Love, love is a verb,
Csus2
Love is a doing word,
G5   D8
Fearless on my breath.

Gentle impulsion,
Csus2
Shakes me, makes me lighter,
G5   D8
Fearless on my breath.

Chorus 1
Csus2
Teardrop on the fire,
G5   D8
Fearless on my breath.

Link ‖: D8 | D8   :‖

© Copyright 1998 Universal/Island Music Limited (50%)/Sony/ATV Music Publishing (UK) Limited (50%).
All rights in Germany administered by Universal/MCA Music Publ. GmbH.
All Rights Reserved. International Copyright Secured.

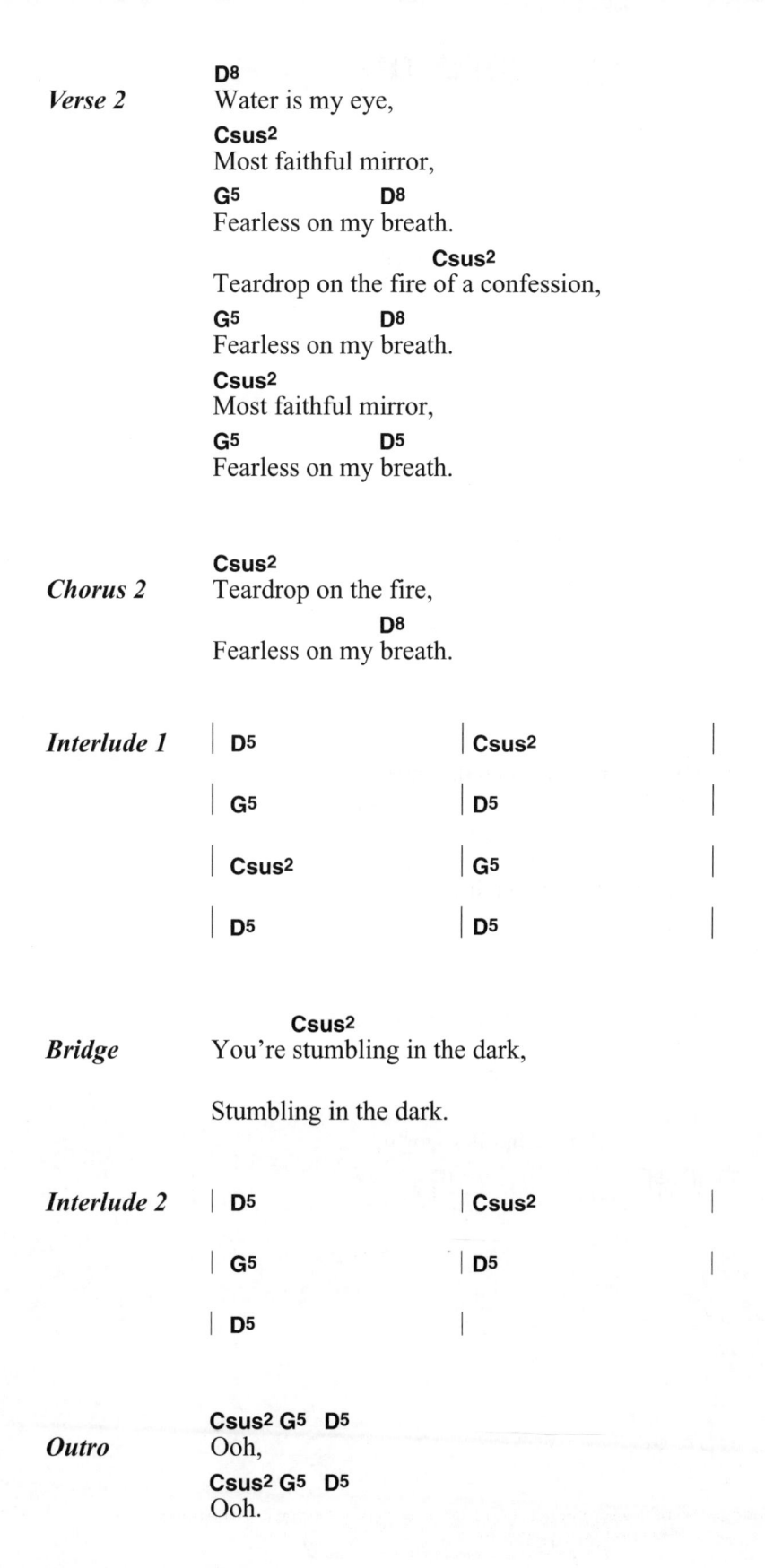

Verse 2

      D8
Water is my eye,
  Csus2
Most faithful mirror,
G5   **D8**
Fearless on my breath.
                        Csus2
Teardrop on the fire of a confession,
G5   **D8**
Fearless on my breath.
Csus2
Most faithful mirror,
G5   **D5**
Fearless on my breath.

Chorus 2

Csus2
Teardrop on the fire,
             D8
Fearless on my breath.

Interlude 1

D5	**Csus2**	
G5	**D5**	
Csus2	**G5**	
D5	**D5**	

Bridge

      Csus2
You're stumbling in the dark,

Stumbling in the dark.

Interlude 2

D5	**Csus2**	
G5	**D5**	
D5		

Outro

Csus2 G5 D5
Ooh,
Csus2 G5 D5
Ooh.

Tell Me What It's Worth

Words & Music by
Devon Hynes

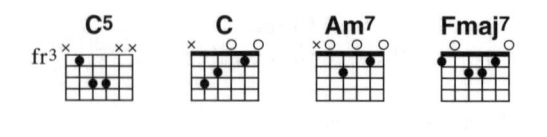

C5   C   Am7   Fmaj7

Intro   ‖: C5 | C5   :‖

Verse 1
    C   Am7
Crack open the good times,
                        C
On a street corner busting rhymes,
                     Am7
But you fell between the lines.
   C   Am7
They all laugh, become a joke,
                       C
Am I crazy baby? Let's all hope.
                           Am7
For narrow halls and crunching drums,

I got the sweets, sugar but that's all.

Chorus 1
   Fmaj7   C
Tell me what it's worth,
   Fmaj7   C
Tell me what it's worth.

© Copyright 2007 Domino Publishing Company Limited (PRS).
All Rights Reserved. International Copyright Secured.

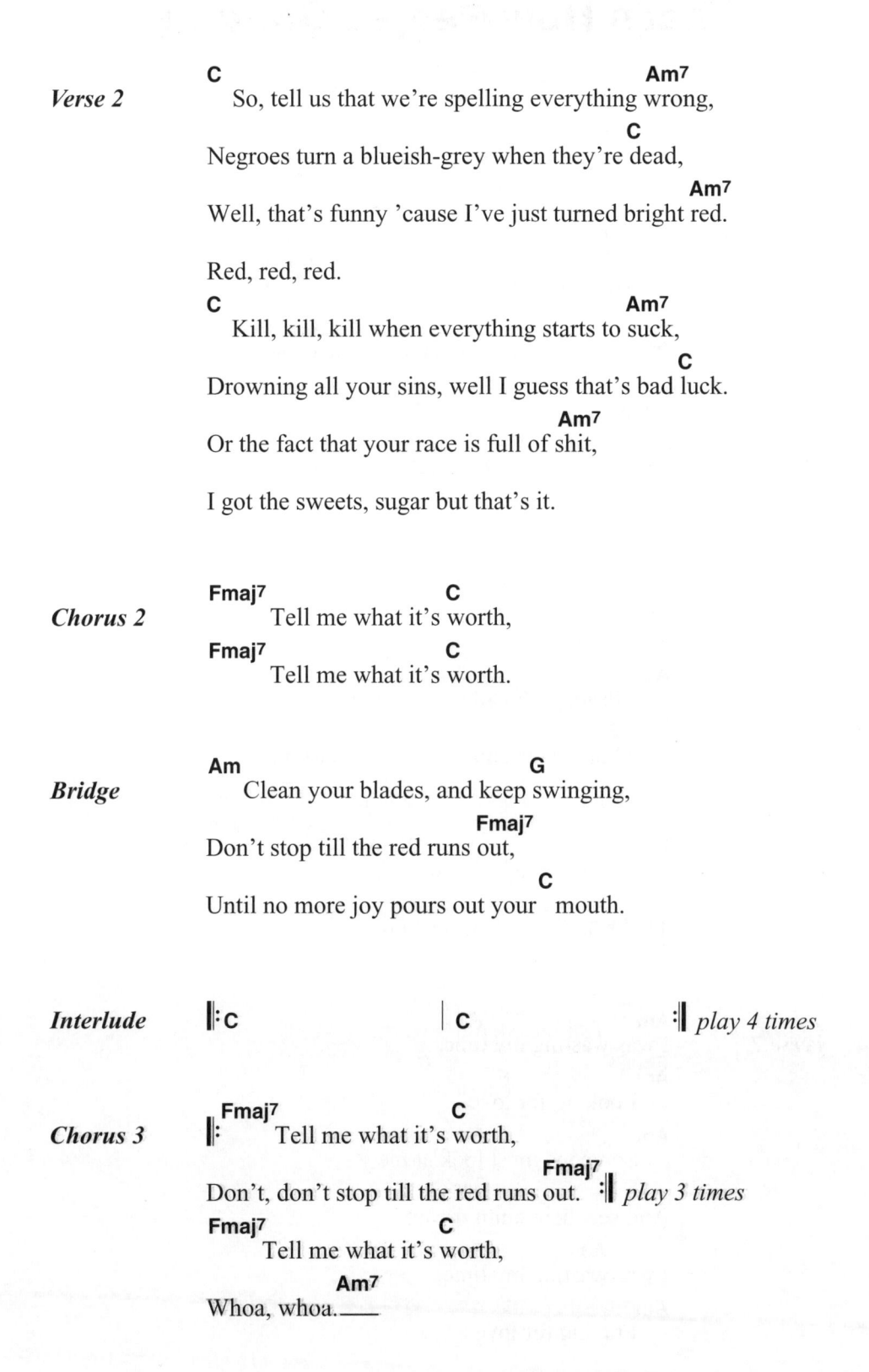

Verse 2

       C   Am7
So, tell us that we're spelling everything wrong,
                                    C
Negroes turn a blueish-grey when they're dead,
                                            Am7
Well, that's funny 'cause I've just turned bright red.

Red, red, red.
     C   Am7
Kill, kill, kill when everything starts to suck,
                                         C
Drowning all your sins, well I guess that's bad luck.
                                Am7
Or the fact that your race is full of shit,

I got the sweets, sugar but that's it.

Chorus 2

     Fmaj7   C
        Tell me what it's worth,
     Fmaj7   C
        Tell me what it's worth.

Bridge

     Am   G
        Clean your blades, and keep swinging,
                                Fmaj7
Don't stop till the red runs out,
                                    C
Until no more joy pours out your mouth.

Interlude   ‖: C | C   :‖ *play 4 times*

Chorus 3

    Fmaj7   C
‖:   Tell me what it's worth,
                               Fmaj7
Don't, don't stop till the red runs out. :‖ *play 3 times*
    Fmaj7   C
      Tell me what it's worth,
         Am7
Whoa, whoa.___

That's How People Grow Up

Words & Music by
Steven Morrissey & Martin Boorer

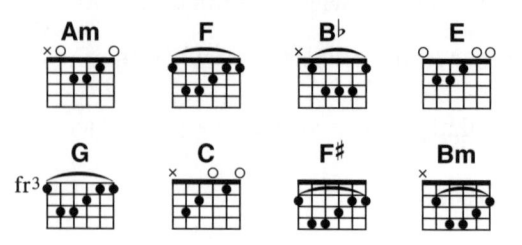

To match recording tune all strings down one tone

Intro ||: Am | F :|| *play 3 times*
| B♭ | E |

Verse 1
Am   F
I was wasting my time,
Am   F
Trying to fall in love.
Am   F
  Disappointment came to me,
  B♭   E
And booted me and bruised and hurt me.

Chorus 1
F   G   C Am
That's how people grow up,—
F   G   E
That's how people grow up.

Verse 2
Am   F
I was wasting my time,
Am   F
  Looking for love.
Am   F
  Someone must look at me,
  B♭   E
And see their sunlit dream.
    Am   F
I was wasting my time,
Am   F
  Praying for love,

© Copyright 2007 Warner/Chappell Music Publishing (50%)/
Sanctuary Music Publishing Limited (50%).
All Rights Reserved. International Copyright Secured.

cont.
    Am   **F**
    For a love that never comes,
    C   **E**
From someone who does not exist and…

Chorus 2   As Chorus 1

Bridge
C   **F♯**   **Bm**
Let me live before I die,___
G   **F♯ G F E**
Not me, not I.___

Verse 3
    Am   **F**
I was wasting my life,
      Am   **F**
Always thinking about my - self.
Am   **F**
Someone on their deathbed said,
      B♭   **E**
"There are other sorrows too;
    Am   **F**
I was driving my car,
  Am   **F**
I crashed and broke my spine.
  Am   **F**
So yes, there are things worse in life,
    C   **E**
Than never being someone's sweetie."

Chorus 3
F   **G**   **C Am**
That's how people grow up,
F   **G**   **E**
That's how people grow up.
F   **G**   **C Am**
That's how people grow up,
F   **G**   **E G**
That's how people grow up.

Outro
C   **F♯**   **Bm**
  As for me, I'm ok,
G   **F♯** **G F E**
  For now, anyway.___

Time To Pretend

Words & Music by
Andrew Vanwyngarden & Benjamin Goldwasser

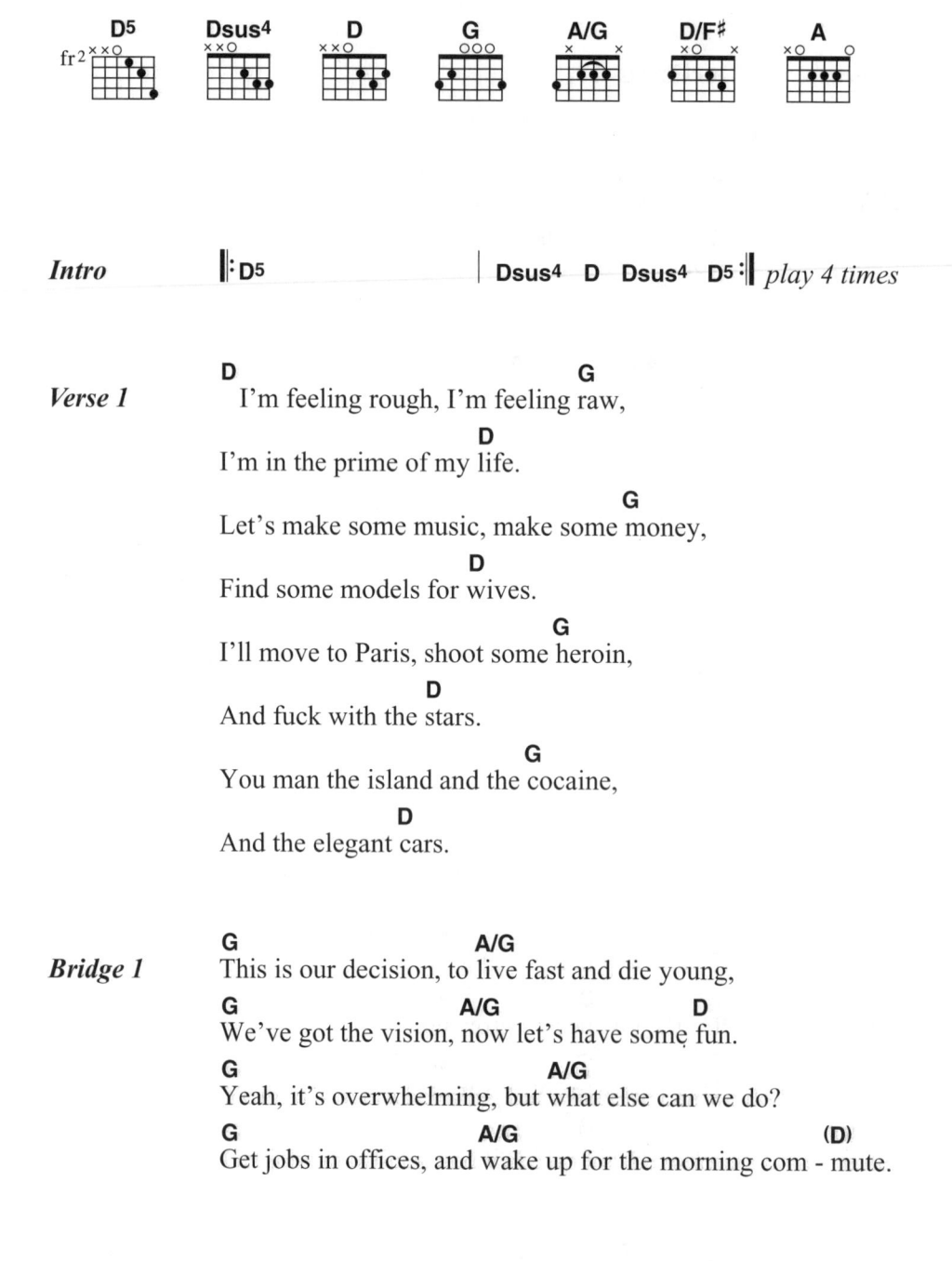

D5 Dsus4 D G A/G D/F# A

Intro ||: D5 | Dsus4 D Dsus4 D5 :|| *play 4 times*

Verse 1
    D   G
I'm feeling rough, I'm feeling raw,
                  D
I'm in the prime of my life.
                               G
Let's make some music, make some money,
                 D
Find some models for wives.
                            G
I'll move to Paris, shoot some heroin,
                 D
And fuck with the stars.
                              G
You man the island and the cocaine,
                D
And the elegant cars.

Bridge 1
    G   A/G
This is our decision, to live fast and die young,
    G   A/G   D
We've got the vision, now let's have some fun.
    G   A/G
Yeah, it's overwhelming, but what else can we do?
    G   A/G   (D)
Get jobs in offices, and wake up for the morning com - mute.

© Copyright 2008 Universal Music Publishing Limited.
All rights in Germany administered by Universal Music Publ. GmbH.
All Rights Reserved. International Copyright Secured.

Link 1 | D | D |
              (- mute)
              | D | D |

Chorus 1
    A   D/F♯
Forget about our mothers and our friends,
          G   A   D
We're fated to pre - tend.
 G   D
  To pre - tend,
        G   D
We're fated to pre - tend,
 G   D   G
  To pre - tend,

Verse 2
  D   G
  I'll miss the playgrounds and the animals,
              D
And digging up worms.
                     G
I'll miss the comfort of my mother,
               D
And the weight of the world.
                    G
I'll miss my sister, miss my father,
         D
Miss my dog and my home.
                           G
Yeah, I'll miss the boredom and the freedom,
            D
And the time spent a - lone.

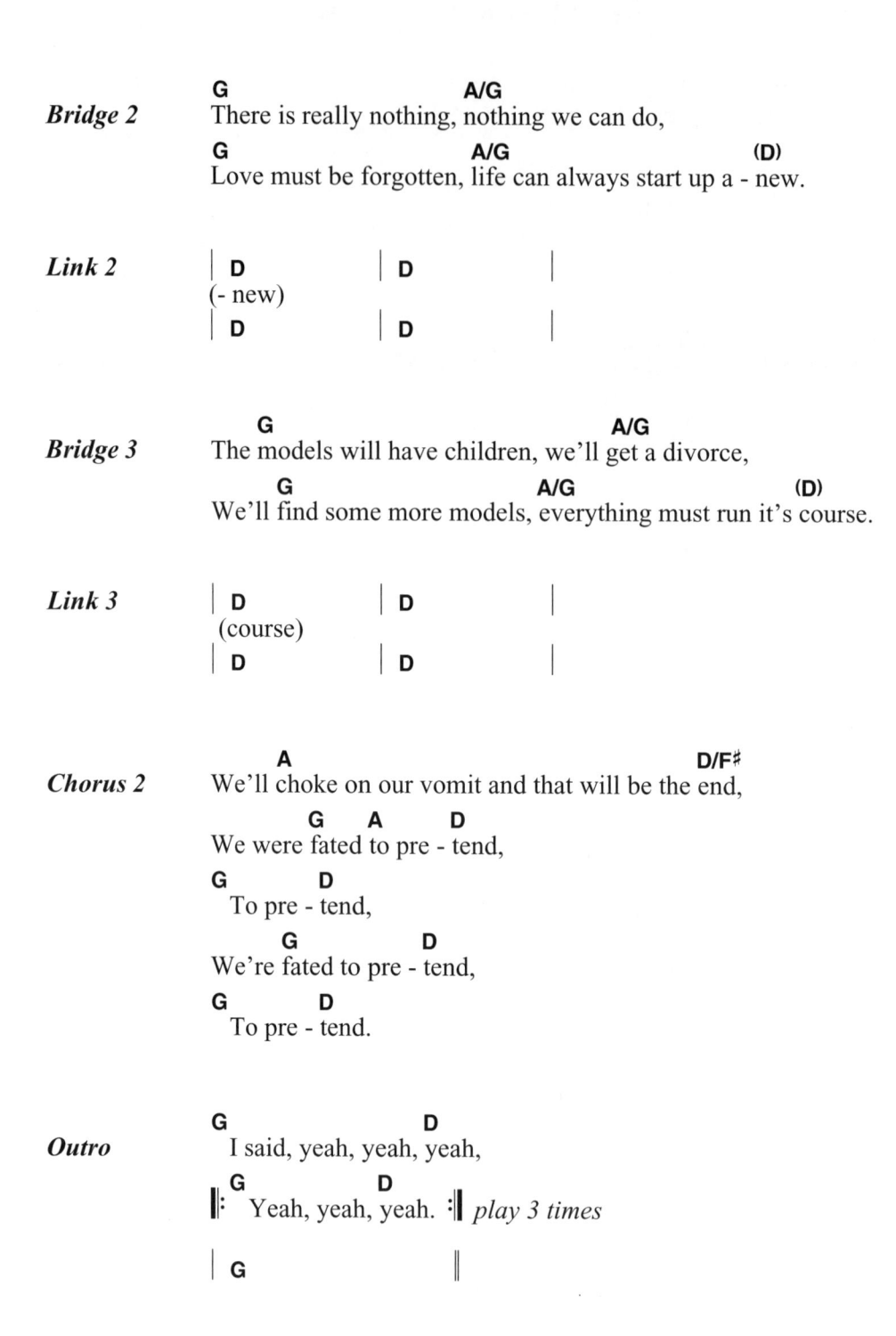

Bridge 2   G   A/G
        There is really nothing, nothing we can do,
        G   A/G   (D)
        Love must be forgotten, life can always start up a - new.

Link 2 | D | D |
        (- new)
        | D | D |

Bridge 3   G   A/G
        The models will have children, we'll get a divorce,
        G   A/G   (D)
        We'll find some more models, everything must run it's course.

Link 3 | D | D |
        (course)
        | D | D |

Chorus 2   A   D/F#
        We'll choke on our vomit and that will be the end,
         G A D
        We were fated to pre - tend,
        G   D
          To pre - tend,
          G   D
        We're fated to pre - tend,
        G   D
          To pre - tend.

Outro   G   D
          I said, yeah, yeah, yeah,
          G   D
        ||: Yeah, yeah, yeah. :|| *play 3 times*

        | G ||

Tranquilize

Words & Music by
Brandon Flowers, Dave Keuning, Mark Stoermer & Ronnie Vannucci

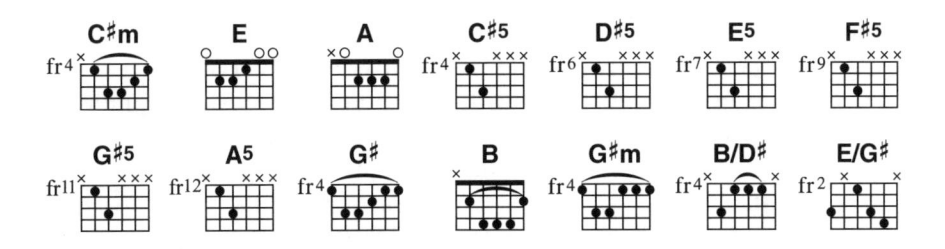

Intro

||: (C#m) | (C#m) :||

||: C#m | C#m :||

Verse 1

C#m
  Time it tells, living in my home town,

Wedding bells they begin easy.

Live it down, baby don't talk that much,

Baby knows, but baby don't tease me.
E
  In the park we could go walking,
A
Drowned in the dark or we could go sailing,
C#m
  On the sea.

Always here, always on time,

Close call, was it love or was it just easy?

Money talks when people need shoes and socks,

Steady boys, I'm thinking she needs me.
E   A
I was just sipping on something sweet,

I don't need political process.

© Copyright 2007 Universal Music Publishing Limited.
All rights in Germany administered by Universal Music Publ. GmbH.
All Rights Reserved. International Copyright Secured.

101

Pre-Chorus 1

     C#5   D#5
   I got this feeling that they're gonna break down the door,
E5   F#5   G#5   A5
   I got this feeling they they're gonna come back for more.
C#5   D#5
   See I was thinking that I lost my mind,
E5   F#5   G#5 A5
   But it's been getting to me all this time,
      G#
And it don't stop dragging me down.

Chorus 1

    E   B   C#m   A
Silently re - flection turns my world to stone,
    E   B   C#m   G#m
Patiently cor - rection leaves us all a - lone.
     A   B
And sometimes I'm a travel man,
      C#m   B   A B
But to - night this engine's fail - ing,
  (E)
And I still hear the children playing.

Verse 2

  C#m
     Kick the can, kick the can, skip and blackjack,

Steal a car and ring a round-rosey.

Rock and roll, candyland, boogeyman,

Run away and give me your sneakers.

Acid rain, when Abel looked up at Cain,

We began the weeping and wailing.

A hurry-high from pestilence pills and pride,

It's a shame, we could have gone sailing.
E   A
   But heaven knows, heaven knows every - thing, tranquilize.

Pre-Chorus 2
     C#5   D#5
I got this feeling that they're gonna break down the door,
E5   F#5   G#5   A5
I got this feeling they they're gonna come back for more.
C#5   D#5
See I was thinking that I lost my mind,
E5   F#5   G#5 A5
But it's been getting to me all this time,
    G#
And it don't stop dragging me down.

Chorus 2
  E   B   C#m   A
Silently re - flection turns my world to stone,
E   B   C#m   G#m
Patiently cor - rection leaves us all a - lone.
   A   B
And sometimes I'm a travel man,
  C#m   B   A B
But to - night this engine's fail - ing,
  (E)
And I still hear the children playing.
                E
Dead beat dancers come to us and stay.

Outro
  B/D#   C#m
'Cause I don't care where you've been,
 B   E/G#
And I don't care what you've seen.
  C#m   F#m
We're the ones who still believe,
 B   E
And we're looking for a page,
 B/D#   C#m
In that lifeless book of hope,
 B   G#m
Where a dream might help you cope,
 C#m   F#m
With the Bushes and the bombs,
 B   E
Uh-huh, Tranquilized.

Valentine

Words & Music by
Richard Hawley

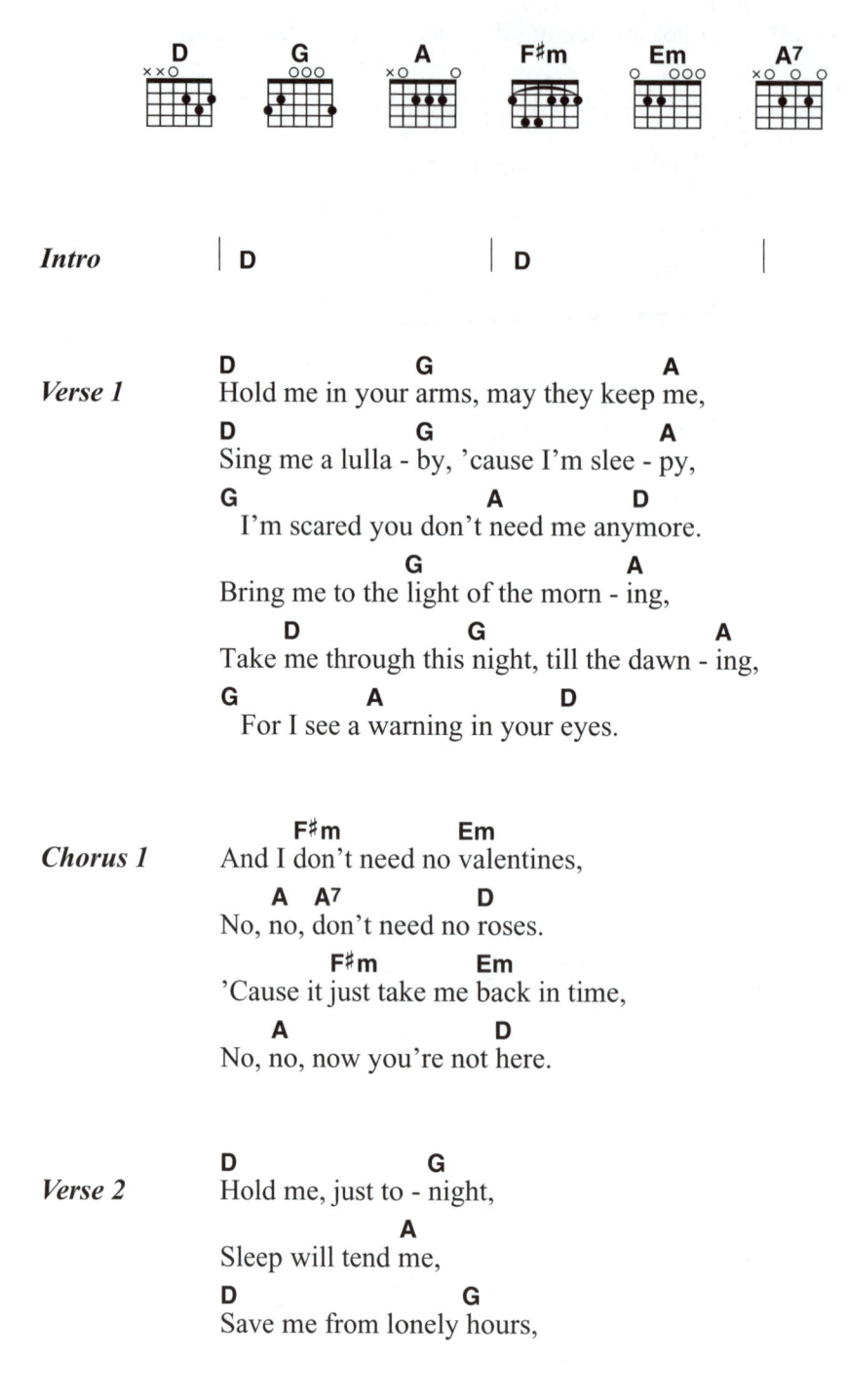

D **G** **A** **F♯m** **Em** **A7**

Intro | D | D |

Verse 1
    D   G   A
Hold me in your arms, may they keep me,
    D   G   A
Sing me a lulla - by, 'cause I'm slee - py,
  G   A   D
  I'm scared you don't need me anymore.
               G   A
Bring me to the light of the morn - ing,
    D   G   A
Take me through this night, till the dawn - ing,
  G   A   D
  For I see a warning in your eyes.

Chorus 1
    F♯m   Em
And I don't need no valentines,
  A A7   D
No, no, don't need no roses.
    F♯m   Em
'Cause it just take me back in time,
  A   D
No, no, now you're not here.

Verse 2
  D   G
Hold me, just to - night,
        A
Sleep will tend me,
  D   G
Save me from lonely hours,

© Copyright 2007 Universal Music Publishing MGB Limited.
All Rights in Germany Administered by Musik Edition Discoton GmbH
(A Division of Universal Music Publishing Group).
All Rights Reserved. International Copyright Secured.

	A
cont.	There's so man - y,

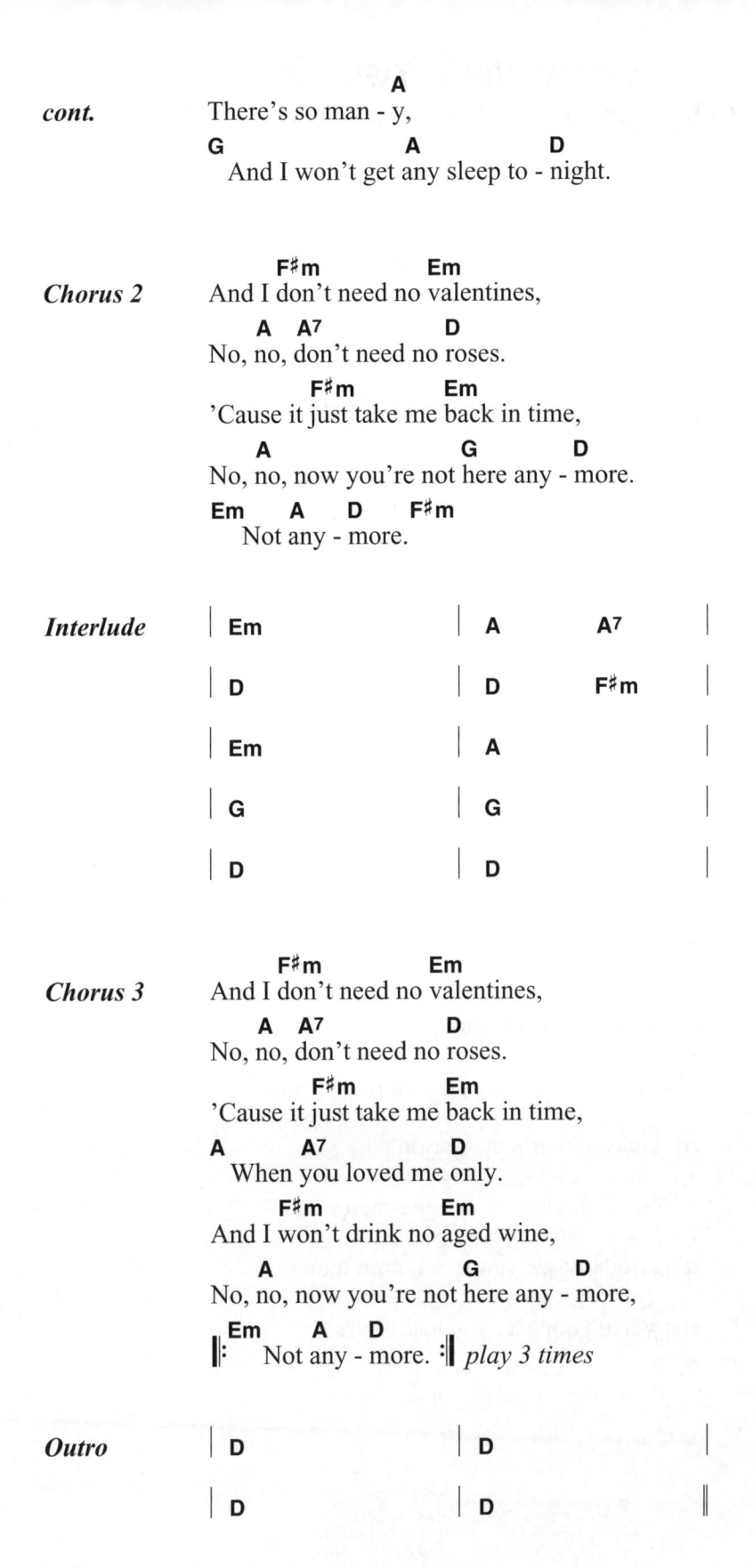

          G   A   D
And I won't get any sleep to - night.

Chorus 2

         F♯m   Em
And I don't need no valentines,
   A A7   D
No, no, don't need no roses.
        F♯m   Em
'Cause it just take me back in time,
   A   G   D
No, no, now you're not here any - more.
Em   A   D   F♯m
   Not any - more.

Interlude

Em	A A7
D	D F♯m
Em	A
G	G
D	D

Chorus 3

        F♯m   Em
And I don't need no valentines,
   A A7   D
No, no, don't need no roses.
        F♯m   Em
'Cause it just take me back in time,
A   A7   D
   When you loved me only.
       F♯m   Em
And I won't drink no aged wine,
   A   G   D
No, no, now you're not here any - more,
 Em   A   D
‖: Not any - more. :‖ *play 3 times*

Outro

| D | D |
| D | D   ‖

What Will You Do
(When The Money Goes)?

Words & Music by
Joseph Carnall, Louis Carnall, Joseph Green & Thomas Rowley

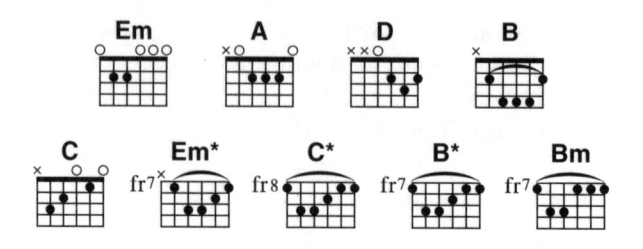

[Chord diagrams: Em, A, D, B, C, Em*, C*, B*, Bm]

Intro

Em	A
D	B
Em	C
D	B
|: Em	Em :|

Verse 1

Em
  I can see a darker side,

I can see it in your eyes.

Maybe things have happened in your life,

And maybe that's the reason why,
 A   D   B
  You're playing for a one-man side.
 Em   C
It's alright when you're winning though,
 D   B
But when you lose, you lose alone.

© Copyright 2007 Universal Music Publishing Limited.
All rights in Germany administered by Universal Music Publ. GmbH.
All Rights Reserved. International Copyright Secured.

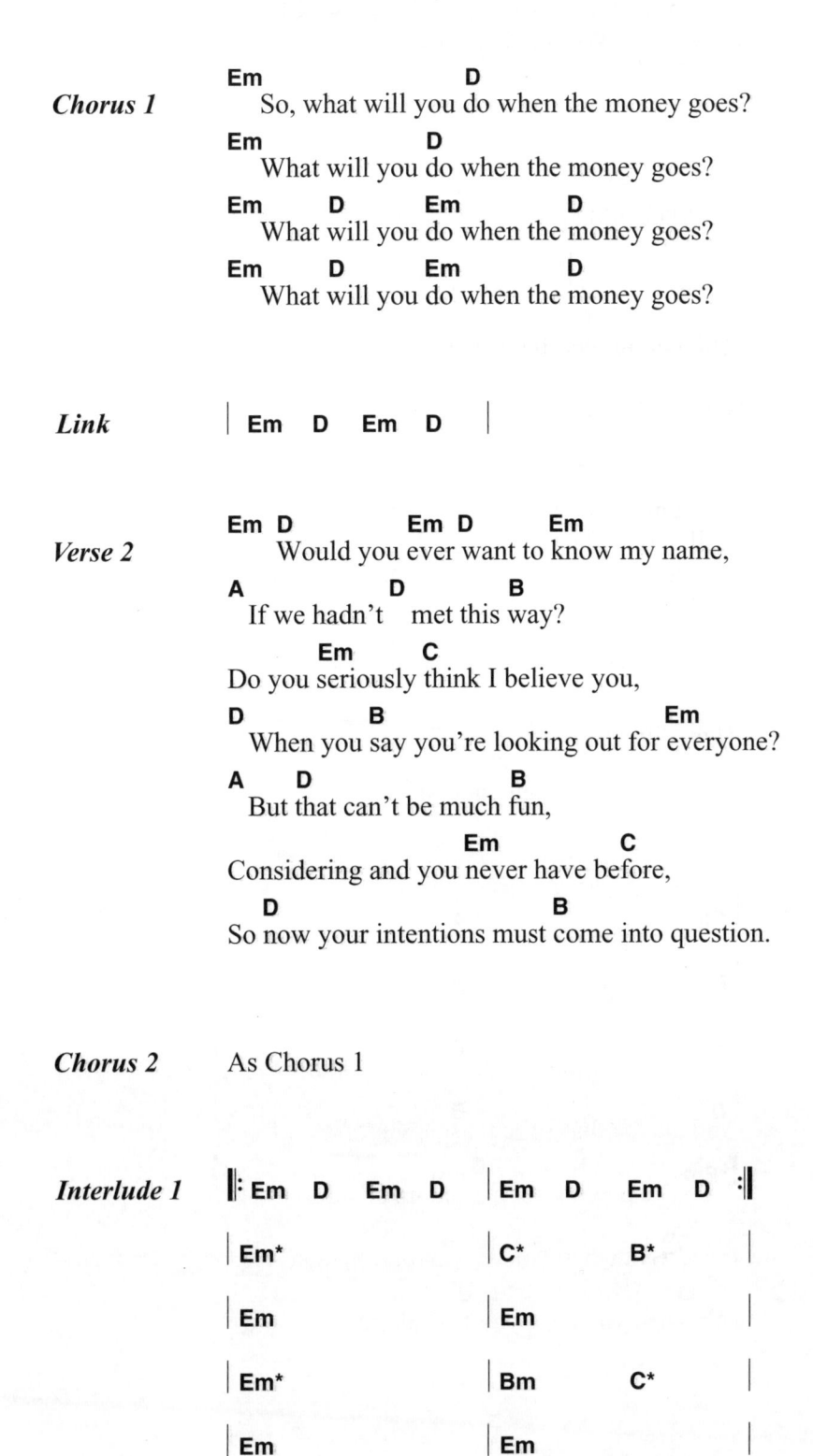

Chorus 1
      Em   D
So, what will you do when the money goes?
      Em   D
What will you do when the money goes?
      Em   D   Em   D
What will you do when the money goes?
      Em   D   Em   D
What will you do when the money goes?

Link | Em D Em D |

Verse 2
Em D   Em D   Em
   Would you ever want to know my name,
A   D   B
  If we hadn't   met this way?
            Em   C
Do you seriously think I believe you,
D   B   Em
  When you say you're looking out for everyone?
A   D   B
  But that can't be much fun,
                    Em   C
Considering and you never have before,
D   B
So now your intentions must come into question.

Chorus 2   As Chorus 1

Interlude 1 |: Em D Em D | Em D Em D :|

                | Em* | C*   B* |

                | Em | Em |

                | Em* | Bm   C* |

                | Em | Em |

Chorus 3

      Em   C   D
When all has disap - peared,
               B
What will you do when the money goes?
Em   C   D
And nothing left but souve - nirs,
              B
What will you do when the money goes?

Bridge

      Em   C   D   B
Will that be the moment when you rea - lise?
      Em   C   D   B
Will that be the moment when you rea - lise?
      Em   C   D   B
Will that be the moment when you rea - lise,
  C
That you,
B
   Had better change your ways.

Interlude 2

Em	A	
D	B	
Em	C	
D	B	
: Em	Em	:

Verse 3
          Em
        I can see a darker side,

I can see it in your eyes,

Maybe things have happened in your life,

And maybe that's the reason why,
A   **D**   **B**
  You're playing for a   one-man side,
Em   **C**
It's alright when you're winning though,
   D   **B**   **(Em)**
But when you lose,   you lose a - lone.

Interlude 3   ‖: **Em**   **C** | **D**   **B** |
                  (- lone.)
             | **Em**   **C** | **D**   **B**   :‖
                                                    (You lose a -

Outro   **Em**   **C**   **D**   **B**
          ‖: Will that be the moment when you rea - lise?   :‖ *play 8 times*
        a - lone.)   (You lose

                      Em
        You lose a - lone.

Worried About Ray

Words & Music by
Alan Gordon, Garry Bonner, Irwin Sparkes, Alan Sharland & Martin Skarendahl

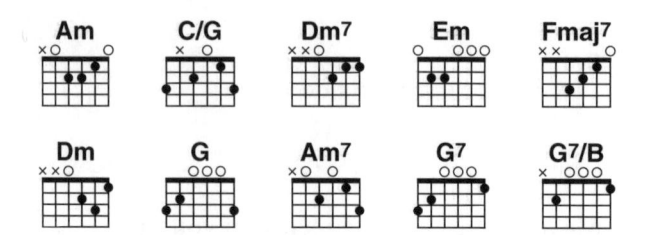

| Am | C/G | Dm7 | Em | Fmaj7 |
| Dm | G | Am7 | G7 | G7/B |

Intro | Am | Am |
            | C/G | C/G |
            | Dm7 | Em |
            | Am | Am |

Verse 1
     Am
Truth be told, the truth be told,
          C/G
I'm worried what the future holds, the future holds,
 Dm7   **Em**   **Am**
I'm starting to worry about Ray.

Truth be told, the truth be told,
          C/G
I'm worried about the future holds, the future holds,
 Dm7   **Em**   **Am**
I'm seriously worried about Ray.

Chorus 1
  Fmaj7   **Dm**
‖: They say the future's out to get you,
  G   **Am7** **G7**
You know that I won't let you fall. :‖

© Copyright 2007 Trio Music Company Incorporated, USA/Alley Music Corporation, USA/
Windswept Trio Music Company Limited/Robbins Music Corporation Limited.
Sony/ATV Music Publishing (UK) Limited (66.66%)/Windswept Trio Music Company Limited (16.67%)/
Robbins Music Corporation Limited (16.67%).
All Rights Reserved. International Copyright Secured.

Interlude 1 | Am | Am |
          | C/G | C/G |
          | Dm7 | Em |
          | Am | Am |

Verse 2

    Am
Truth be told, the truth be told,
            C/G
I'm treading on my tippy toes, my tippy toes,
  Dm7   Em   Am
I'm starting to worry about Ray.

The truth be told, the truth be told,
            C/G
I'm treading on my tippy toes, my tippy toes,
  Dm7   Em   Am
I'm painfully so worried about Ray.

Chorus 2

  Fmaj7   Dm
They say the future's out to get you,
    G   Am7   G7
You know that I won't let you fall.
  Fmaj7   Dm
They say the future's out to get you,
    G   Am7   G7/B
You know that I won't let you fall.

Interlude 2 | Fmaj7 | Fmaj7 |
               | Dm | G |
               | Am7 | G7 |
               | Fmaj7 | Fmaj7 |
               | Am7 | G7 |

Chorus 3
```
       Fmaj7                        Dm
   ‖: They say the future's out to get you,
         G              Am7    G7
     You know that I won't let you fall. :‖
       Fmaj7                        Dm
   ‖:     The future's out to get you,
            Em    G     Am7    G7
     The future's out to get you, oh. :‖
```

Link   ‖: Am | Am   :‖

Outro
```
     Am
     Truth be told, the truth be told,
                        C/G
     I'm worried what the future holds, the future holds,
            Dm7          Em           Am
     I'm so tired of being worried about Ray.
```